BREADMAKER'S GUIDE
Savory & Sweet Recipes
from Around the World

BREADMAKER'S GUIDE

*Savory & Sweet Recipes
from Around the World*

JAN THOMSON

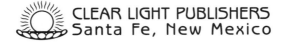
CLEAR LIGHT PUBLISHERS
Santa Fe, New Mexico

Dedication

To my husband, David, the love of my life and my best friend.
To my sister Liz, my other best friend, for all her help.
To my mother-in-law Edith for doing such a good job raising her son.
To my Mom for having the patience to let her four-year-old daughter
help her make bread—
Thanks for the memories.

Acknowledgments

Once again to the nicest group of people you could hope to work with.
Thank you Harmon Houghton, Marcia Keegan, Sara Held, and the rest
of the folks at Clear Light Publishers. You are the best.

Copyright © 2000 Jan Thomson
Clear Light Publishers, 823 Don Diego, Santa Fe, NM 87501
WEB: www.clearlightbooks.com

First Edition 10 9 8 7 6 5 4 3 2 1

Library of Congress Cataloging-in-Publication Data
Thomson, Jan, 1952–
    Breadmaker's guide: savory & sweet recipes from around the world / Jan Thomson.
        p. cm.
    Includes index.
    ISBN 1-57416-049-4
    1. Cookery (Bread) 2. Bread. I. Title.

    TX769.T46 2000
    641.8'15—dc21   00-02381

Cover and bread photographs © David Thomson
Cover design: Carol O'Shea
Typography and design: Carol O'Shea
Printed in Canada

Contents

I
Breadmaking Basics

For me, a complicated recipe is a waste of time. In my years of teaching cooking and collecting and adapting recipes, I've found they can always be made simpler, shorter, and easy to remember so that you can follow them without a roadmap. I thought, wouldn't it be nice to pick up a cookbook, see the ingredients and directions at a glance?—and not have to read through two or three pages of small print, and after an interruption or two, have to read it all again? In both my cookbooks, I've worked hard to simplify.

RECIPE FORMAT FOR
BREADMAKER'S GUIDE

The format for the recipes in this book has been reduced to a simple set of ingredients and summarized instructions. In my 25 years of breadmaking, I've come to use something I call the **Easy Mix Method**. There are only three basic steps to remember:

Mix the **dry ingredients** together.
Mix the **wet ingredients** together.
Mix the **dry ingredients** and **wet ingredients** together to form a dough or batter.

Dry ingredients: I have formatted each recipe to use 3 cups of flour (the amount for 1 loaf) plus yeast and other dry ingredients. A bread machine uses less yeast. In most recipes, yeast for the bread machine recipe is listed as $2\frac{1}{4}$ teaspoons.

Wet ingredients: In the recipes, wet ingredients are listed for the 3 basic breadmaking methods:
no-knead batter bread
hand-kneaded bread
bread made in a bread machine

You can basically use any liquids, as long as they equal the amount specified in each recipe and are the correct temperature. The Easy Mix Method uses a standard 120° for the liquids, unless the recipe indicates otherwise.

Steps in breadmaking: In the next chapter I give the detailed steps for batter breads (pages 12–14) and for hand-kneaded breads (pages 15–18). (When using a bread machine, follow the manufacturer's instructions.) In each recipe you will find a reminder list of steps.

POINTERS FOR BEGINNERS

It's important to set aside enough time so that you won't feel
pushed and you can enjoy yourself. Breadmaking shouldn't be a
chore, but a chance to relax and be creative. Don't rush—have
some fun with it.

After you've decided what kind of bread you want to try, sit
down, relax, enjoy a cup of coffee, and read the **Detailed Steps** in
Chapter 2 twice. After you've made bread a few times, looking at
the reminder list in the recipe will be enough. You'll soon know the
feel, look, and smell of a good dough. Then, if you want more
than one loaf of bread, simply double the recipe. Bread freezes
very well.

Make sure your kitchen work surface is clean and uncluttered.
Run a sink full of soapy water for fast cleanups as you work.

Double-check to see that you have all the ingredients and tools
you'll be using. It's best to put away ingredients as soon as you've
measured out what you need—except for flour and liquid. You may
need to add more of these.

BREADMAKING TOOLS

Large bowl (it should hold at least 8–12 quarts)
A good thermometer (quick or instant read)
Large sturdy wooden spoon
Wire whisk
A sturdy electric mixer
Measuring cups and spoons
A glass, 4–6-cup measuring cup or small pot for heating liquids
Dough cutter/scraper for dividing the dough and scraping your
    work surface
A rubber spatula
Pastry brush—the kind that looks like a paintbrush (the others are
    too stiff)

Timer

A large saltshaker with a handle to spread the flour evenly on your
   work surface.

Loaf pans (9 x 5 and 8 x 4)

Flat pans or cookie sheets for shaped breads

Rolling pin

Wire cooling racks

A sharp bread knife

Razor blade for slashing the dough (handles for double-sided blades
   are sold at kitchen stores)

ABOUT YEAST

Yeast is a microscopic, unicellular plant (a fungus) that feeds on
sugar. It reproduces rapidly under the right conditions of warmth
and moisture if some form of sugar is available. The most notice-
able effect of yeast is the production of carbon dioxide, which
expands the dough and makes the baked bread light and porous.

   The no-knead yeast batter bread and kneaded bread recipes in
this book call for active dry yeast. It can be bought in small packets
that need no refrigeration. If bought in bulk, it should be kept in a
cool, dry place. Most bread machine manufacturers suggest a spe-
cific type of yeast for their particular machine, some calling for
quick-rise yeast.

   Proper temperature of wet ingredients is essential to make yeast
grow. A liquid that is too hot can kill the yeast; too cool a liquid can
retard its growth. I strongly recommend using a quick-read or instant-
read thermometer to eliminate guesswork when preparing the liquids
for breadmaking. At some point you may learn just by touch.

FLOURS USED IN BREADMAKING

A general note about flour: Always keep a small amount of flour and liquid available so that final adjustments for moisture content can be made, whether kneading by hand, electric mixer, or bread machine. The reason is that there are many factors that contribute to the ability of flour to absorb moisture, including the age and type of flour, weather, and altitude. After making a few loaves of bread, you'll learn how the dough should feel and look, and you can tell in the beginning stages of mixing when to add more flour or liquid. You do not have to be a master baker.

All the recipes in this book call for *bread flour,* which in my opinion turns out the best-textured product, but in a pinch a good *all-purpose flour* will do. For a bread that is high in protein, see Cornell Bread, page 36.

There has been much controversy over the health implications of bleached flour, and it has been banned in several countries. Bleaching or brominating makes the flour whiter and adds to the shelf life. Unbleached flour, after being stored for several months, undergoes a natural oxidation, which is harmless but reduces the whiteness of the flour. Unbleached flour gives a slightly creamy color to the bread.

All the flours used in this book can be easily found in the grocery store or local health food store. It is fun to mix and match flours for new tastes and textures. When mixing flours, you need to include a flour with a high gluten content because gluten gives the elasticity to dough that makes it rise well. Bread flour (bleached or unbleached) has the highest gluten content and produces a light, porous bread. When using a low-gluten flour, such as rye or whole wheat, I prefer to use 2 cups of bread flour to 1 cup of whole grain flour for a lighter, less dense loaf. If you like a denser, chewier bread, experiment with using a larger proportion of whole grain flour.

Different flours and grains add various characteristics to bread. The following table describes the types of grains and flours that are used in breads and indicates the proportions I recommend for combining them with white bread flour.

Type of flour	Portions	Information
Bread flour, bleached or unbleached	3 cups bread flour	Milled from the endosperm of hard red spring wheat, bread flour is high in gluten (a protein).
All-purpose flour, bleached and unbleached	3 cups all-purpose flour	Milled from a combination of hard spring wheat and soft winter wheat, it is a multipurpose flour with slightly less gluten than bread flour.
Whole wheat flour	1 cup whole wheat flour 2 cups bread flour	Milled from the entire wheat kernel (bran, germ, and endosperm), it may undergo a small amount of cleaning and sifting. For breadmaking select whole wheat *bread* flour (hard spring wheat, such as Deaf Smith County wheat), *not* whole wheat *pastry* flour (from soft winter wheat).
Stone-ground whole wheat flour	1 cup stone-ground flour 2 cups bread flour	A coarser grind of whole wheat flour, it contains larger grain particles and will produce a heavier, coarser crumb.
Rye flour Pumpernickel flour	1 cup dark or light rye flour (or 1 cup pumpernickel flour) 2 cups bread flour	Rye flour is milled from the entire rye berry and is low in gluten. Pumpernickel flour is also milled from the whole rye grain but has a coarser texture than regular rye flour.

Type of flour	Portions	Information
Semolina flour Durum flour	½ cup semolina flour ½ cup durum flour 2 cups bread flour	Semolina and durum are both milled from the very hardest variety of spring wheat, but semolina flour is less fine than durum. Semolina flour is high in protein and is used mostly for making pasta.
Graham flour	1 cup graham flour 2 cups bread flour	Graham flour is 100% whole wheat flour that has not been sifted or cleaned. (Don't confuse graham flour with the graham cracker, which derives its flavor from sweeteners.)
Wheat germ	Add 2–3 tablespoons + a few drops of liquid if needed	The embryo of the wheat berry (kernel), wheat germ has a high percentage of oil and must be kept refrigerated. Used raw or toasted, it adds a nutty flavor and is a good source of vitamins and minerals.
Gluten flour	Add 1–2 tablespoons + a few drops of liquid if needed	Bread flour to which extra gluten has been added, gluten flour may be added when you are using a flour that is low in gluten to give a lighter texture. It is usually found in health food stores.
Cracked wheat	1 cup cracked wheat flour 2 cups bread flour	Wheat berries that have been toasted, then crushed.
Cornmeal	1 cup cornmeal 2 cups bread flour	Cornmeal can be ground from the "degerminated" or whole corn kernels (the latter is more nutritious).

Type of flour	Portions	Information
Rolled oats	1 cup rolled oats 2–2½ cups bread flour	When oats are ground, the bran and germ are left intact. Oats are high in protein, B vitamins, and vitamin E.
Oat bran	¼ cup per 1 cup bread flour	The outer covering of the oat grain, oat bran adds moisture and nutrients. It should be kept refrigerated
Wheat bran	¼ cup per 1 cup bread flour	Bran is the outer hull of the wheat kernel and adds texture, fiber, and a nutty flavor. It should be kept refrigerated.
Rice flour	1 cup rice flour 2 cups bread flour	A low-gluten flour, it is usually found in health food stores.
Millet flour	1 cup millet flour 2 cups bread flour	Millet is a tiny grain known for easy digestion and high protein content.
Potato flour	1 cup potato flour 2 cups bread flour	Made from cooked potatoes, dried and ground into flour, it is usually available from health food stores.
Buckwheat flour	1 cup buckwheat flour 2 cups bread flour	Buckwheat is very high in protein and rich in B vitamins and vitamin E.

WHAT ARE NO-KNEAD YEAST BATTER BREADS?

Not to be confused with quick breads, which use baking powder or baking soda as the leavening agent, these breads have a whole different taste and crumb. Like quick breads, though, no-knead yeast batter breads are too wet to knead.

The lost art of no-knead batter breads was redeveloped and refined in the mid to late 1940s. Once in a while you will come across a few good no-knead batter bread recipes, but usually in the yellowing pages of your grandmother's favorite cookbook. The old no-knead batter breads were usually very high in fat, but I have found that in most cases high fat is not necessary.

Busy home cooks will find no-knead yeast batter breads especially appealing because they are quicker and easier to make than kneaded breads. Beating the batter takes less time and effort than kneading, and most batter breads require only one short rise (about 45 minutes). The batter is wet enough to be easily beaten by hand or with an electric mixer. A no-knead batter bread can be prepared quickly for a last-minute meal. Your home will be filled with that wonderful home-baked yeast bread aroma.

These breads are also appealing because of their nice open crumb. They are excellent for sandwiches and toast, and they keep very well.

II
Tips and Techniques

ADJUSTING FOR ALTITUDE
AND WEATHER

High altitude: The most common problem in baking at altitudes above 5,000 feet is the sunken loaf. Because air pressure at higher altitudes is less than at sea level, the dough meets less resistance as it rises. It can therefore rise too high, weaken, and collapse. There are various ways to adjust your baking to high altitude. For kneaded breads, you can increase liquids by 1–2 tablespoons. For bread machines, see guidelines on page 24. For any type of bread, you can add one tablespoon of pure gluten (found in the refrigerated section of most health food stores). Extra gluten will strengthen the dough and make it more elastic so that it is less likely to fall if it rises higher than normal.

Whatever else you do, be sure to check your dough 10 to 30 minutes sooner than you normally would, depending on the altitude where you are. This is especially important for the last rise, when the dough is shaped and in the pan or on a cookie sheet. For batter breads, watch the rise carefully. If the batter rises too high, you can simply stir it down and let it rise to just one inch below the top of the pan; then put it in the oven to bake.

Dough tends to dry out more quickly at high altitudes, and you may need to add liquid, a few drops at a time. You'll know the moisture is right if the dough is soft and not sticky—it should leave the sides of the bowl clean just before you start to knead. If you grease the dough thoroughly when you put it into the oiled bowl, it will be less likely to dry out. Wrapping your bread well after baking and cooling will also help keep it moist at high altitudes.

Weather: Weather does indeed affect baking, and adjusting to weather conditions is basically a matter of common sense. Since warmth makes yeast more active, be sure to find a spot for the rising that doesn't overheat on very hot days. Otherwise it may rise too high or too quickly and then collapse. On cold days, be sure the rising dough is protected from drafts and is placed in a spot where you know it will stay warm. If you live where desert-like conditions are normal, you should check your dough for dryness and add a teaspoon of liquid at a time, as needed. If summertime humidity is high, begin by using 2 tablespoons less liquid and add it back little by little if the dough is too dry.

IS IT DONE YET?

There's nothing like a hot slice of fresh bread right out of the oven and dripping with butter. But there's nothing worse than cutting into a beautiful hot loaf that is half cooked and gooey in the middle.

To test for doneness, most cookbooks tell you to tap the loaf to see if it sounds hollow. I have never heard a hollow sound come from a loaf of bread. I go by smell, color, and weight, but the surest method is to use a quick-read thermometer. Insert the thermometer into the center of the loaf. When the bread is done, the thermometer will read 200–215° degrees.

If the sides have not browned as much as you'd like, take the loaf out of the pan and place it directly on the rack in the oven. Let it bake another 5 minutes—no longer or it may dry out.

A note on oven temperature: I have found in all my years of baking bread only one oven that gave a correct temperature reading. That stove was the price of a new Buick. The best thing to do is get yourself an oven thermometer (even if you think your oven is reliable) and make adjustments accordingly. Oven thermometers are available in supermarkets and department stores.

BATTER BREADS

Detailed Steps for No-Knead Yeast Batter Bread

Mix
- Mix the dry ingredients together with a wire whisk.
- Mix the wet ingredients together with a wire whisk (if needed).
- Heat the wet ingredients to 120°, checking the temperature with a quick-read thermometer.

- Mix the dry and wet ingredients together using your hands or electric mixer, adding more flour or liquid, if needed, until well incorporated.
- Beat until the batter becomes springy. (Remember, if a batter is too wet to be kneaded, it will be sticky.)

If the recipe calls for only one rise, proceed as follows:

1st rise
- Using cooking spray, spray an 8 x 4 inch loaf pan.
- Turn dough out into a loaf pan and let rise to one inch from the top of the pan (30–45 minutes).
- Sprinkle with seeds of your choice (optional).
- Bake immediately, following instructions below for final step.

If the recipe calls for a 2nd rise, proceed as follows:

1st rise
- Cover the bowl and let the bread rise for 45 minutes.
- Stir down—stir the dough with a wooden spoon about 15 times to deflate the dough for the 2nd rise.

2nd rise
- Using cooking spray, spray an 8 x 4 inch loaf pan.
- Turn dough out into a loaf pan and let it rise one inch from the top.
- Sprinkle with seeds of your choice (optional).

Bake, test for doneness, and cool
- Bake for the time and at the temperature given in the recipe. Average baking time: 45–50 minutes.
- Test for doneness using a quick-read thermometer inserted into the middle of the loaf. It should read 200–215°.
- Remove from pan and cool on a wire rack in an upright position.

Summary of Steps for Batter Breads

Mix

1st rise

Stir down, 2nd rise

Bake

Test for doneness and cool

These steps are listed as a reminder with each recipe.

Tricks to Remember When Making No-Knead Batter Breads

- You can use your hands, a wooden spoon, or an electric mixer. I have found that using my hands takes less effort than using a spoon.
- Press the batter down evenly in the loaf pan using an oiled rubber spatula. You can also smooth the top with your oiled fingers. I have found that using oil instead of flour makes it easier to smooth the batter in the pan.
- Never let the batter rise over the top of the pan. Letting it rise too high can cause the loaf to fall during baking. If it rises too high, turn the batter back into the bowl, beat it another 15 times, and let it rise to one inch below the top of the pan. (Or you can just stir it down thoroughly in the pan, and let it rise again.)
- Cool the bread on a wire rack in an upright position, not on its side.

HAND-KNEADED BREADS

Detailed Steps for Hand-Kneaded Breads

Mix

- Mix the dry ingredients together with a wire whisk and set aside.
- Mix the wet ingredients together with a wire whisk (if necessary).
- Heat to 120°, checking the temperature with your quick-read thermometer.
- Put the flour in the bowl and make a hole in the middle of the flour. This is called a well. Pour the warmed wet ingredients in the center.
- With warm hands, start with a swirling motion to incorporate the wet and the dry ingredients, working more flour into the dough from the sides.
- Continue to mix until the dough leaves the sides of the bowl, adding more flour if needed or warm liquid, a few drops at a time.
- Keep mixing until the dough is smooth.

Or use an electric mixer: A heavy-duty mixer, such as a KitchenAid, with a dough hook is the best tool for mixing the dough thoroughly. Mine is 23 years old and works like new.

Mix

- Using your electric mixer, place the dry ingredients in the mixing bowl and mix together with the dough hook.
- Mix the wet ingredients together (if necessary).
- Heat to 120°. Check temperature, using your quick-read thermometer.
- Add the warmed wet ingredients to the dry ingredients and turn mixer on low.

- Let the dough hook mix the dough until it leaves the sides of the bowl, adding flour if needed or warmed liquid, a few drops at a time.
- Keep mixing until the dough is smooth.

Knead: Kneading can be very relaxing and therapeutic, so have some fun.

- Spread an even amount of flour over your work surface to keep the dough from sticking. Turn out the dough (lay the dough) on your floured work surface.
- Fold the dough over on itself. Using the palm of your hands, press it down, give it a quarter turn, fold it over again, and press it down.
- Repeat until the dough is smooth and takes on an elastic quality—it should spring back when you pinch up a piece of it. If the dough hasn't reached this point, keep kneading.

Oil bowl, 1st rise

- Pour a bit of oil in the bottom of the bowl. Using a paper towel, coat the sides of the bowl with a thick, dripping layer of oil. Place the dough in the bowl, and rotate the dough so that all sides are covered with oil. The oil keeps the dough from drying out. Cover bowl with a large dishtowel or a bath towel.
- For the dough to rise, you need a warm environment free of drafts. I like to place the dough in my gas oven with just the pilot light on. I have also used the top of the TV while it is on or the top of the refrigerator. Maintain the warmth so the yeast will keep growing.
- Let the dough double in bulk. Set your timer for one hour, then check the dough. If it has not doubled in size, set the timer for another 45 minutes to 1 hour.
- The first rise will take 1 to 2 hours for most breads.

Punch down, 2nd rise

- With your fist, punch the dough in the center to deflate it.

- Lightly flour your work surface (too much flour will make streaks in the finished product). Start the kneading process again, working the dough 25–30 times.
- Place the dough in the bowl, and let it rise until it has doubled in bulk.
- Rising time for the 2nd rise varies with each recipe. On average it will take 45 minutes to 1 hour.

Note: If the recipe does not call for a 2nd rise, after the 1st rise shape the dough as described below and go on to the next step.

Shape into a loaf, 3rd rise
(As you handle the dough to shape it, it will deflate.)
- Shape the dough in the manner the recipe calls for or choose your own. Directions on how to shape breads are on pages 20–21.
- Spray the pan with cooking spray (even if your pan is the non-stick variety), and place your dough in the pan. Fill only one-half the loaf pan because the dough will rise again.
- Let your dough rise until it reaches just over the top of the loaf pan.
- Rising time for the 3rd rise typically is 30 to 40 minutes.

Bake, test for doneness, and cool
- Make sure the oven is fully preheated. Bake for the time and temperature given in the recipe. Average baking time: 25–30 minutes.
- To test for doneness, most cookbooks tell you to thump the bottom of the loaf to see if there is a hollow sound. I have never been able to hear a hollow sound, so I go by the smell, look, and weight. But the best way to tell if a loaf of bread is done is by using your quick-read or instant thermometer to test for doneness. Stick the thermometer into the middle of the loaf. It should read 200–215° degrees.
- Remove the bread from the pan. Place it on its side on a wire rack to cool. Always let the loaf cool completely before storing it in a plastic bag; otherwise it will sweat and become soggy.

Summary of Steps for Hand-Kneaded Breads

Mix, knead, oil bowl

1st rise

Punch down, 2nd rise

Shape into a loaf, 3rd rise

Bake

Test for doneness and cool

These steps are listed as a reminder with each recipe.

Troubleshooting for Hand-Kneaded Breads

The trouble	Cause / solution
Dough does not rise.	Too little yeast or yeast too old. Liquids too hot or too cold. Too little time allowed for dough to rise.
Dough is stiff and hard to knead.	Too much flour: try kneading water into the dough a few drops at a time.
Dough is too soft.	Not enough flour: knead in more flour a sprinkle at a time (this sometimes causes streaking).
Loaf has a crater when baked.	Dough too wet: more flour is needed.
Loaf is gummy inside and/or too dark on the outside.	Lower oven temperature and bake loaf longer. If loaf browns too quickly, make a tent by draping aluminum foil (sprayed with cooking spray) over the loaf for the first 10–15 minutes of baking. The foil will protect the loaf and keep it from browning too much.

The trouble	Cause / solution
Bottom of loaf is burnt.	Oven not fully preheated. Oven rack too low: bake loaf in the middle of the oven.
Top of loaf is burnt.	Oven rack placed too high.
Crust has split.	Top should have been slashed.
Loaf is an odd shape.	Seams were not pinched together tightly enough to close.
Crust has pulled away from the loaf.	The top of the loaf was allowed to dry out during the final rising. If top begins to look dry, spray it lightly with cooking spray.
Crust has browned unevenly.	Caused by hot spots (uneven temperatures) in the oven: use a foil tent sprayed with cooking spray for the first 10 to 15 minutes of baking; or try turning the bread around mid-baking.
A large crack around the crust.	Dough is too dry: add 1–2 tablespoons more liquid. Dough did not rise enough during baking: check baking time, oven temperature, and temperature of wet ingredients.
Mushroom tops (lumps on crust).	Crumbly dough that was too dry: reduce flour (rather than add more liquid). Dough is too wet: reduce moist ingredients. Too little salt. Too much yeast (Dough rose too high in the pan).
Crust too crisp.	Too much fat was used. Use milk instead of water. Place baked loaf in a plastic bag.
Crust tough (or too chewy).	Use more milk than water. Brush loaf with melted butter while still hot. Place loaf in a plastic bag when cooled.

HOW TO SHAPE BREAD

Most dough can be made into any shape you want. You may use any recipe for kneaded breads for making anything from a baguette to a bialy. If the recipe calls for braiding and you are not in the braiding mood, shape the dough into a loaf, being careful to follow the basic cooking times for loaves.

Basic loaf shape: Flatten out dough slightly. Start to roll up (squeezing out any large bubbles) the long way, paying attention to the size of your pan. Pinch the seams shut along the bottom and the ends, and place the seam side down in the loaf pan. The dough should fill the loaf pan only half way. Always spray the loaf pan with cooking spray even if it is a non-stick pan.

Braided and braided circle: Divide the dough into 3 equal amounts and shape them into 3 long snakes by rolling them on your work surface with your hands. Pinch the three ends together. Start braiding by laying one strip over the other until you have run out of dough. Pinch the open ends together to seal. Join the two ends to make a round braid. Seal the round loaf by pinching the ends together and folding the end under the loaf to hide it.

Slashing a loaf: If you are making a traditional shape such as a French bread, it is important to slash the top of the loaf so that it will not split during baking. This is done after you have shaped the dough and just before the last rise. Make 3 or 4 diagonal slashes according to the length of the loaf. The slashes should be about ½ inch deep. I recommend using a razor blade for a clean cut that does not pull or tear the loaf. See list of tools, page 4.

French or Italian loaf: Follow the directions for the basic loaf, but shape so that it is longer and narrower and make 4 or 5 diagonal slashes. I recommend using a French loaf baking pan to help keep the loaf shape. You can also use rolled-up dishtowels that have been floured (on the sides that touch the dough) to support the sides of the dough during the 3rd rise.

Long flattened loaf: Follow the directions for the basic loaf, but shape it longer and narrower. With a rolling pin, roll it lightly about $\frac{3}{4}$ inch thick. Make 4 or 5 diagonal slashes.

Oval: Shape the dough as if you were making a regular loaf but shape it into an oval.

Round: Shape into a round ball, flatten slightly, and slash an X 2 x 2 inches long and at least $\frac{1}{4}$–$\frac{1}{2}$ inch deep in the center of the loaf.

Baguettes and bread sticks: Divide your dough into 3 pieces and start rolling the dough into long snakes, making 6–8 slashes $\frac{1}{2}$ inch deep. To make bread sticks, roll them thinner. Use the very chewy crust for best results (see p. 22).

Extra crisp bread sticks: Roll them even thinner.

Note: French baguette and bread stick pans are a wise investment. Using these special pans will help keep the shape of the loaf during the final rise. Also, they are made in a way that will help produce a nice crust. You can find them in most kitchen stores. The pan will come with instructions for use.

French Pullman: With almost any recipe you can use a Pullman loaf pan. It comes with a lid that keeps the dough from rising above the top and gives a dense close crumb to the bread. Before the 3rd rise, spray the Pullman pan with cooking spray, shape the dough into a regular loaf shape, put it in the pan, and cover it with the lid. Be sure to spray the inside of the lid. Bake according to pan directions.

HOW TO CREATE THE CRUST YOU PREFER

Type of crust	Ingredients	Directions
Crisp	Cold water in a spray bottle	Spray the loaf 4 times during baking.
Soft	Milk Or Melted butter	Brush with milk **before** baking. Brush with melted butter **after** baking.
Shiny	Egg wash: 1 beaten egg mixed with 1 tablespoon milk or water Or 1 teaspoon cornstarch and ¼ cup boiling water	Brush on egg wash before baking. Mix cornstarch and water and let thicken. Brush on before baking.
Topping of rolled oats or nuts, seeds, onions, or olives, chopped coarsely	Egg wash (see above) Topping of your choice	Before baking, brush with egg wash, sprinkle with topping, and brush with egg wash again, using a patting motion. This keeps the seeds or topping in place, like a glue.
Fine Topping	Egg wash (see above) Pepper, cornmeal, or Parmesan cheese	Before baking, brush with egg wash and sprinkle with topping.
Chewy	6 to 8 ice cubes	Steaming: place an old pan on the floor of the oven. Preheat oven to full heat. Toss ice cubes into the pan, place the loaf in right away, closing the door quickly.
Very chewy	Egg wash: (see above)	Before baking, brush with egg wash. Then steam (follow directions for chewy crust).

Type of crust	Ingredients	Directions
Flour	Egg wash: 1 beaten egg mixed with 1 tablespoon milk or water Flour	Before last rise, brush lightly with egg wash, and dust heavily with flour. Slash top. Steam (follow directions for chewy crust).
Shredded cheese	Shredded cheese (your choice)	Sprinkle with cheese the last 10 minutes during baking.

BREAD MACHINES

I was disappointed with the first bread machine I purchased, but that was many years ago. Since then, bread machines have been improved greatly.

Your bread machine comes with instructions for adding ingredients. Follow the manufacturer's instructions carefully. The instructions will include a list of basic ingredients for very basic breads. Over the years I've been asked to adapt a variety of bread recipes for bread machines. I became interested in finding a standard way of adapting different kinds of recipes. With some experimentation, I found the key and have provided adaptations for every recipe in this book that can be made with a bread machine.

Tips and Troubleshooting for Bread Machines

Problem solving: Although the manufacturer's instructions generally provide reliable information for basic breads, you may need additional information to help you avoid problems with the crust or the loaf if you try different types of bread with your machine. You may also need to know how to adapt bread machine baking for high altitudes and different weather conditions. The guidelines below will work with most bread machines.

Adjusting for high altitude: Some adjustments should be made for baking at high altitudes—5,000 feet or more above sea level. I have even needed adjustments at 3,700 feet. The most common problem is loaves that sink during baking. The lower air pressure at high altitudes provides less resistance to the rising of the dough. The loaf therefore can rise too high and then collapse.

Here are some basic guidelines: The easiest preventive measure is to set your machine for the rapid-bake cycle so that the loaf won't have time to rise too high. Or increase your liquids by 1–2 tablespoons. Or reduce the yeast from $2\frac{1}{4}$ to $1\frac{1}{8}$ teaspoons. Increasing the salt will also inhibit the rise, but most people do not want the added salt. For the recipes in this book, you can add one tablespoon of gluten (found in the refrigerated section of most health food stores). Gluten is the sticky protein that makes bread hold together when it rises; extra gluten makes the dough more elastic so that it can rise high without collapsing during baking.

Flour tends to dry out at high altitudes, so you might need less flour or more liquid.

How the weather affects your bread machine and what to do. For the most part, I had to learn the hard way. Here in Montana we have extreme weather changes, from 40° below zero to 105° above and a wide range in between on the same day. This chart will help you figure out what to expect from different weather conditions and how to cope with them.

Weather	What to do
Dryness	If dough looks dry while kneading, add liquid a teaspoon at a time.
High humidity	Decrease the liquid by 2 tablespoons, adding liquid back if the dough looks too dry.
Cold weather	Be extra careful to keep bread machine in a warm place and free from drafts.
Hot weather	The dough can rise too fast and too high. Keep bread machine in a cool place and check the rise 10–15 minutes early.

Crust problems can often be traced to weather or to ingredient amounts.

Problems with crusts	Cause / solution
A large crack around the crust	Dough is too dry: add 1–2 tablespoons more liquid. Dough did not rise enough during baking: check baking time and temperature of wet ingredients.
Mushroom tops (lumps on crust)	Crumbly dough that was too dry: reduce flour (rather than add more liquid). Dough is too wet: reduce moist ingredients such as vegetables—they add moisture to the dough. Too much dough for your machine. Too little salt. Too much yeast. Try rapid-bake cycle. Too much sugar or too many sweet ingredients. Using an instant or fast-rising yeast.
Burnt crust	Use the light setting for the crust. Remove from bake cycle early. Use less sugar.
Blisters on the crust	Not enough rising time.

Problems with crusts	Cause / solution
Doughy spots on the crust	Too much dough for the machine. Too many heavy ingredients for the short cycle. Too much fat.
Large air bubble in the center of the crust	Dough was too dry: add 1–2 tablespoons liquid. Dough poorly mixed by machine.
Crust too crisp	Too much fat was used. Use milk instead of water. Place baked loaf in a plastic bag. Let bread cool in the machine with the lid closed.
Crust too soft	Use water instead of milk. Remove from the bread pan as soon as the bake cycle is over. Do not store loaf in plastic bag until it has cooled completely.
Crust tough (or too chewy)	Use more milk than water. Brush loaf with melted butter while still hot. Place loaf in a plastic bag when cooled. Let loaf cool in the bread machine or use the cool-down cycle.

Problems with loaves	Cause / solutions
Small loaf—the # 1 problem	Checklist: 1. Did you forget the yeast? 2. Were your liquids too hot/cold? 3. Did you add too much salt/forget the sugar? 4. Were the dry ingredients too cold? 5. Did you remember the preheat cycle (if applicable)? 6. Did you add the yeast, then the salt? 7. If it's cold, is your bread machine in a warm spot? 8. Did your ingredients mix well? 9. Did you open the lid too many times? 10. Did you forget the mixing blade? Another possible cause: too much fat.

Problems with loaves	Cause / solutions
Pale loaf	Use the dark setting for the crust. Use more sugar.
Holes in the loaf	Too little salt. Dough too wet: use less liquid.
Loaf with collapsed or soft sides	Dough too wet. Loaf left in the pan too long.
Crumbly or coarse loaves	Too much whole grain or cereal. Dough too dry. Lack of salt.
Dry loaf	Use less (or no) egg.
A loaf dense and heavy enough for a doorstop	Don't forget the mixing blade.
Scary-shaped loaves	All of the above.

III
White Loaf Breads

Use bleached or unbleached flour, whichever you prefer. Bread flour has more gluten than all-purpose flour and will make a more elastic dough and lighter bread. All the bread recipes are for an 8 x 4 inch loaf pan and will make one loaf. However, kneaded breads can be shaped into a loaf of your choice. No-knead batter breads require a loaf pan to hold their shape.

Note: Each recipe lists a separate amount of yeast—$2\frac{1}{4}$ tea-spoons—for using with bread machines. The other amount of yeast is for no-knead batter breads and hand-kneaded breads.

Baking times are given in each recipe for no-knead batter bread and hand-kneaded bread. When using a bread machine, fol-low the manufacturer's directions.

Basic White Bread
with Non-Fat Option

Dry ingredients

3 cups bread flour
1 tablespoon yeast
  (2¼ teaspoons for bread
  machines)
1 teaspoon salt
1 tablespoon sugar

Wet ingredients for
batter bread

1¾ cups water
1 tablespoon oil (optional)

Wet ingredients for
kneaded bread

1 cup water
1 tablespoon oil (optional)

Wet ingredients for
bread machines

1⅛–1¼ cups water as required
1 tablespoon oil (optional)

Steps for batter bread

Mix
1st rise
Stir down
Bake at 375° for 50 minutes
Test for doneness and cool

Steps for kneaded bread

Mix, knead, oil bowl
1st rise
Punch down, 2nd rise
Shape into a loaf, 3rd rise
Crust: soft
Bake at 400° for
  25–30 minutes
Test for doneness and cool

Crust: soft
Brush loaf with milk *before* baking.
  Or
Brush loaf with melted butter *after* baking.

Sesame Seed Bread

Dry ingredients
3 cups bread flour
1 tablespoon yeast
    (2$\frac{1}{4}$ teaspoons for bread
    machines)
1 teaspoon salt
1 tablespoon sugar
4 tablespoons toasted
    sesame seeds

**Wet ingredients for
batter bread**
1$\frac{3}{4}$ cups water
2 tablespoons sesame seed oil

**Wet ingredients for
kneaded bread**
1 cup water
2 tablespoons sesame seed oil

**Wet ingredients for
bread machines**
1 cup + 2 tablespoons water
2 tablespoons sesame seed oil

Steps for batter bread
Mix
1st rise
Stir down, 2nd rise
Bake at 375^0 for 50 minutes
Test for doneness and cool

Steps for kneaded bread
Mix, knead, oil bowl
1st rise
Punch down, 2nd rise
Shape into loaf, 3rd rise
Crust: sesame seeds
Bake at 400^0 for 25 minutes
Test for doneness and cool

Crust: topping of sesame seeds
Prepare egg wash: Mix 1 beaten egg with
1 tablespoon milk or water. Before baking,
brush with egg wash, sprinkle with topping,
and brush with egg wash again, using a
patting motion.

Lemon Pepper Bread with Chives

Dry ingredients
3 cups bread flour
1 tablespoon yeast
(2¼ teaspoons for bread
machines)
1 teaspoon salt
1 tablespoon sugar
¼ cup lemon pepper
½ cup fresh chives, chopped
and loosely packed

**Wet ingredients for
batter bread**
1¾ cups water
1 tablespoon olive oil

**Wet ingredients for
kneaded bread**
1 cup water
1 tablespoon olive oil

**Wet ingredients for
bread machines**
1⅛–1¼ cups water as required
1 tablespoon olive oil

Steps for batter bread
Mix
1st rise
Stir down, 2nd rise
Bake at 375° for 50 minutes
Test for doneness and cool

Steps for kneaded bread
Mix, knead, oil bowl
1st rise
Punch down, 2nd rise
Shape into loaf, 3rd rise
Crust: lemon pepper
Bake at 400° for 25 minutes
Test for doneness and cool

Crust: topping of lemon pepper
Prepare egg wash: Mix 1 beaten egg with 1
tablespoon milk or water. Before baking, brush
with egg wash and sprinkle with topping.

Hungarian White Bread

Dry ingredients

3 cups bread flour

1 tablespoon yeast
(2¼ teaspoons for bread
machines)

1 teaspoon salt

1 tablespoon sugar

½ teaspoon each anise seed
and fennel seed, crushed

**Wet ingredients for
batter bread**

1¾ cups water

2 tablespoons olive oil

**Wet ingredients for
kneaded bread**

1 cup water

2 tablespoons olive oil

**Wet ingredients for
bread machines**

1 cup + 2 tablespoons water

2 tablespoons olive oil

Steps for batter bread

Mix

1st rise

Stir down, 2nd rise

Bake at 375° for 50 minutes

Test for doneness and cool

Steps for kneaded bread

Mix, knead, oil bowl

1st rise

Punch down, 2nd rise

Shape into a loaf, 3rd rise

Crust: soft

Bake at 400° for 25 minutes

Test for doneness and cool

Crust: soft
Brush loaf with milk *before* baking.
  Or
Brush loaf with melted butter *after* baking.

English Muffin Bread

Dry ingredients
3 cups bread flour
$\frac{1}{4}$ teaspoon baking soda
1 tablespoon yeast
  ($2\frac{1}{4}$ teaspoons for bread
  machines)
1 teaspoon salt
2 tablespoons sugar

Wet ingredients for batter bread
$1\frac{3}{4}$ cups buttermilk
1 tablespoon melted butter

Wet ingredients for kneaded bread
1 cup buttermilk
1 tablespoon melted butter

Wet ingredients for bread machines
1 cup + 2 tablespoons
  buttermilk
1 tablespoon melted butter

Steps for batter bread
Mix
1st rise
Stir down, 2nd rise
Bake at 375° for 50 minutes
Test for doneness and cool

Steps for kneaded bread
Mix, knead, oil bowl
1st rise
Punch down, 2nd rise
Shape into a loaf, 3rd rise
Crust: soft
Bake at 400° for 25 minutes
Test for doneness and cool

Variation: You can add 2 tablespoons of Italian seasoning for something different.

Crust: soft
Brush loaf with milk *before* baking.
  Or
Brush loaf with melted butter *after* baking.

Buttermilk, Bran, and Wheat Germ Bread

Dry ingredients
2½ cups bread flour
¼ cup each, bran and
    toasted wheat germ
1 tablespoon yeast
    (2¼ teaspoons for bread
    machines)
1 teaspoon salt

**Wet ingredients for
batter bread**
1¾ cups buttermilk
2 tablespoons honey
1 tablespoon olive oil

**Wet ingredients for
kneaded bread**
1 cup buttermilk
2 tablespoons honey
1 tablespoon olive oil

**Wet ingredients for
bread machines**
1 cup + 2 tablespoons
    buttermilk
2 tablespoons honey
1 tablespoon olive oil

Steps for batter bread
Mix
1st rise
Stir down, 2nd rise
Bake at 375⁰ for 50 minutes
Test for doneness and cool

Steps for kneaded bread
Mix, knead, oil bowl
1st rise
Punch down, 2nd rise
Shape into a loaf, 3rd rise
Crust: soft
Bake at 400⁰ for 25 minutes
Test for doneness and cool

Crust: soft
Brush loaf with milk *before* baking.
  Or
Brush loaf with melted butter *after* baking.

Egg Bread

Dry ingredients
3 cups bread flour
1 tablespoon yeast
(2¼ teaspoons for bread
machines)
1 teaspoon salt
1 tablespoon brown sugar

Wet ingredients for batter bread
1½ cups milk
2 eggs, beaten

Wet ingredients for kneaded bread
¾ cup milk
2 eggs, beaten

Wet ingredients for bread machines
1 cup + 1 tablespoon milk
2 eggs, beaten

Steps for batter bread
Mix
1st rise
Stir down, 2nd rise
Bake at 375° for 50 minutes
Test for doneness and cool

Steps for kneaded bread
Mix, knead, oil bowl
1st rise
Punch down, 2nd rise
Shape into loaf, 3rd rise
Crust: melted butter
Bake at 400° for 25 minutes
Test for doneness and cool

Crust: soft
Brush loaf with milk *before* baking.
  Or
Brush loaf with melted butter *after* baking.

Cornell Bread

Cornell University did a study on soy flour and found that it provides excellent nutritional value at a minimal cost. Cornell recommends refrigerating soy flour.

Dry ingredients
2¾ cups bread flour
¼ cup soy flour
1 tablespoon yeast
  (2¼ teaspoons for bread machines)
1 teaspoon salt
1 tablespoon sugar
3 tablespoons dry milk

Wet ingredients for batter bread
1 cup milk
¾ cup water
1 tablespoon melted butter

Wet ingredients for kneaded bread
½ cup milk
½ cup water
1 tablespoon melted butter

Wet ingredients for bread machines
1 cup milk
¼ cup water
1 tablespoon melted butter

Steps for batter bread
Mix
1st rise
Stir down, 2nd rise
Bake at 350° for 50 minutes
Test for doneness and cool

Steps for kneaded bread
Mix, knead, oil bowl
1st rise
Punch down, 2nd rise
Shape into a loaf, 3rd rise
Crust: soft
Bake at 400° for 25 minutes
Test for doneness and cool

Crust: soft
Brush loaf with milk *before* baking.
  Or
Brush loaf with melted butter *after* baking.

ONION BREADS
Onion Bread

Dry ingredients
3 cups bread flour
1 envelope onion soup mix
1 tablespoon yeast
  ($2\frac{1}{4}$ teaspoons for bread
  machines)
1 tablespoon sugar

**Wet ingredients for
batter bread**
$1\frac{3}{4}$ cups water
1 tablespoon olive oil

**Wet ingredients for
kneaded bread**
1 cup water
1 tablespoon olive oil

**Wet ingredients for
bread machines**
$1\frac{1}{8}$–$1\frac{1}{4}$ cups water as required
1 tablespoon olive oil

Steps for batter bread
Mix
1st rise
Stir down, 2nd rise
Bake at 375° for 50 minutes
Test for doneness and cool

Steps for kneaded bread
Mix, knead, oil bowl
1st rise
Punch down, 2nd rise
Shape into a loaf, 3rd rise
Crust: chewy
Bake at 400° for 25 minutes
Test for doneness and cool

Crust: chewy
Steam the loaf: Place a pan on the floor of the oven. Preheat oven to full heat. Toss 6 to 8 ice cubes into the pan, place the loaf in right away, and close the door quickly.

Italian Herb and Onion Bread

Dry ingredients
3 cups bread flour
1 tablespoon yeast
  (2¼ teaspoons for bread
  machines)
1 teaspoon salt
1 tablespoon sugar
3 tablespoons Italian herbs
¼ cup green onions, thinly
  sliced

**Wet ingredients for
batter bread**
1¾ cups water
1 tablespoon oil (optional)

**Wet ingredients for
kneaded bread**
1 cup water
1 tablespoon oil (optional)

**Wet ingredients for
bread machines**
1⅛–1¼ cups water as required
1 tablespoon oil (optional)

Steps for batter bread
Mix
1st rise
Bake at 350° for 50 minutes
Test for doneness and cool

Steps for kneaded bread
Mix, knead, oil bowl
1st rise
Punch down, 2nd rise
Shape into a loaf, 3rd rise
Crust: green onions
Bake at 400° for 25 minutes
Test for doneness and cool

Crust: topping of green onions, chopped
Prepare egg wash: Mix 1 beaten egg with
1 tablespoon milk or water. Before baking,
brush with egg wash, sprinkle with topping,
and brush with egg wash again, using a
patting motion.

Sage and Onion Bread

Dry ingredients
3 cups bread flour
1 tablespoon yeast
 (2¼ teaspoons for bread
 machines)
1 teaspoon salt
1 tablespoon sugar
4 tablespoons fresh sage,
 coarsely chopped and rubbed
 between your fingers to
 release the flavor
1 cup red onion, diced small
 and sauteed in one tablespoon butter and drained

**Wet ingredients for
batter bread**
1¾ cups water
1 tablespoon olive oil

**Wet ingredients for
kneaded bread**
1 cup water
1 tablespoon olive oil

**Wet ingredients for
bread machines**
1⅛–1¼ cups water
1 tablespoon olive oil

Steps for batter bread
Mix
1st rise
Stir down, 2nd rise
Bake at 375° for 50 minutes
Test for doneness and cool

Steps for kneaded bread
Mix, knead, oil bowl
1st rise
Punch down, 2nd rise
Shape into loaf, 3rd rise
Crust: chewy
Bake at 400° for 25 minutes
Test for doneness and cool

Crust: chewy
Steam the loaf: Place a pan on the floor of
the oven. Preheat oven to full heat. Toss 6
to 8 ice cubes into the pan, place the loaf in
right away, and close the door quickly.

Rosemary Red Onion Bread

Dry ingredients
3 cups bread flour
1 tablespoon yeast
  (2¼ teaspoons for bread
  machines)
1 teaspoon salt
1 tablespoon sugar
¼ cup fresh rosemary,
  chopped small and packed
1 cup red onion, diced small

**Wet ingredients for
batter bread**
1¾ cups water
2 tablespoons olive oil

**Wet ingredients for
kneaded bread**
1 cup water
1 tablespoon olive oil

**Wet ingredients for
bread machines**
1 cup + 2 tablespoons water
2 tablespoons olive oil

Steps for batter bread
Mix
1st rise
Stir down, 2nd rise
Bake at 375° for 50 minutes
Test for doneness and cool

Steps for kneaded bread
Mix, knead, oil bowl
1st rise
Punch down, 2nd rise
Shape into loaf, 3rd rise
Crust: very chewy
Bake at 400° for 25 minutes
Test for doneness and cool

Crust: very chewy
Prepare egg wash: Mix 1 beaten egg with 1 tablespoon milk or water. Before baking, brush with egg wash. Then steam: Place a pan on the floor of the oven. Preheat oven to full heat. Toss 6 to 8 ice cubes into the pan, place the loaf in right away, and close the door quickly.

Herb Onion Bread with Sun-Dried Tomato

Dry ingredients
3 cups bread flour
1 tablespoon yeast
  (2¼ teaspoons for bread
  machines)
1 teaspoon salt
1 tablespoon sugar
2 tablespoons each, fresh basil,
  cilantro, oregano, chopped
  small and packed
1 tablespoon garlic, minced
½ cup sun-dried tomatoes,
  chopped very small and
  packed

**Wet ingredients for
batter bread**
1¾ cups water
1 tablespoon tomato paste

**Wet ingredients
kneaded bread**
1 cup water
1 tablespoon tomato paste

**Wet ingredients for
bread machines**
1⅛–1¼ cups water as required
1 tablespoon tomato paste

Steps for batter bread
Mix
1st rise
Stir down, 2nd rise
Bake at 350° for 55–60
  minutes
Test for doneness and cool

Steps for kneaded bread
Mix, knead, oil bowl
1st rise
Punch down, 2nd rise
Shape into loaf, 3rd rise
Crust: chewy
Bake at 400° for 30 minutes
Test for doneness and cool

Crust: chewy
Steam the loaf: Place a pan on the floor of
the oven. Preheat oven to full heat. Toss 6
to 8 ice cubes into the pan, place the loaf in
right away, and close the door quickly.

Egg and Onion Buttermilk Bread

Dry ingredients
3 cups bread flour
1 tablespoon yeast
(2¼ teaspoons for bread
machines)
1 teaspoon salt
1 tablespoon sugar
1 cup green onion, thinly sliced
and packed

**Wet ingredients for
batter bread**
1 cup buttermilk
½ cup milk
2 eggs beaten

**Wet ingredients for
kneaded bread**
½ cup buttermilk
¼ cup milk
2 eggs beaten

**Wet ingredients for
bread machines**
1 cup buttermilk
1 tablespoon milk
2 eggs

Steps for batter bread
Mix
1st rise
Bake at 350° for 50 minutes
Test for doneness and cool

Steps for kneaded bread
Mix, knead, oil bowl
1st rise
Punch down, 2nd rise
Shape into a loaf, 3rd rise
Crust: green onions
Bake at 400° for 25 minutes
Test for doneness and cool

Crust: topping of green onions, chopped
Prepare egg wash: Mix 1 beaten egg with
1 tablespoon milk or water. Before baking,
brush with egg wash, sprinkle with topping,
and brush with egg wash again, using a
patting motion.

Sour Cream and Green Onion Bread

Dry ingredients
3 cups bread flour
1 tablespoon yeast
(2¼ teaspoons for bread
machines)
1 teaspoon salt
1 tablespoon sugar
1 cup green onions, thinly
sliced and loosely packed

**Wet ingredients for
batter bread**
1¾ cups sour cream
1 tablespoon melted butter

**Wet ingredients for
kneaded bread**
1 cup sour cream
1 tablespoon melted butter

**Wet ingredients for
bread machines**
1 cup + 2 tablespoons sour
cream
1 tablespoon melted butter

Steps for batter bread
Mix
1st rise
Stir down, 2nd rise
Bake at 350° for 55 minutes

Steps for kneaded bread
Mix, knead, oil bowl
1st rise
Punch down, 2nd rise
Shape into a loaf, 3rd rise
Crust: chewy
Bake at 400° for 25 minutes
Test for doneness and cool

Crust: chewy
Steam the loaf: Place a pan on the floor of
the oven. Preheat oven to full heat. Toss 6
to 8 ice cubes into the pan, place the loaf in
right away, and close the door quickly.

Black Pepper Green Onion Bread

Dry ingredients
3 cups bread flour
1 tablespoon yeast
  (2¼ teaspoons for bread
  machines)
1 teaspoon salt
1 tablespoon sugar
1 tablespoon coarse ground
  pepper (or to taste)
1 cup green onions, thinly sliced
  (green parts only), packed

Wet ingredients for batter bread
1¾ cups water
1 tablespoon melted butter

Wet ingredients for kneaded bread
1 cup water
1 tablespoon melted butter

Wet ingredients for bread machines
1⅛–1¼ cups water as required
1 tablespoon melted butter

Steps for batter bread
Mix
1st rise
Stir down, 2nd rise
Bake at 375° for 50 minutes
Test for doneness and cool

Steps for kneaded bread
Mix, knead, oil bowl
1st rise
Punch down, 2nd rise
Shape into loaf, 3rd rise
Crust: green onions
Bake at 400° degrees for 25
  minutes
Test for doneness and cool

Crust: topping of green onions, chopped
Prepare egg wash: Mix 1 beaten egg with
1 tablespoon milk or water. Before baking,
brush with egg wash, sprinkle with topping,
and brush with egg wash again, using a
patting motion.

SPICY BREADS
Salsa Bread

Dry ingredients
3 cups bread flour
1 tablespoon yeast
   (2¼ teaspoons for bread
   machines)
1 teaspoon salt
1 tablespoon sugar

Wet ingredients for batter bread
1¾ cups salsa
1 tablespoon olive oil

Wet ingredients for kneaded bread
1 cup salsa
1 tablespoon olive oil

Wet ingredients for bread machines
1¼ cups salsa
1 tablespoon olive oil

Steps for batter bread
Mix
1st rise
Stir down, 2nd rise
Bake at 375° for 55–60
   minutes
Test for doneness and cool

Steps for kneaded bread
Mix, knead, oil bowl
1st rise
Punch down, 2nd rise
Shape into loaf, 3rd rise
Crust: chewy
Bake at 400° for 30 minutes
Test for doneness and cool

Crust: chewy
Steam the loaf: Place a pan on the floor of the oven. Preheat oven to full heat. Toss 6 to 8 ice cubes into the pan, place the loaf in right away, and close the door quickly.

Cajun Bread

Dry ingredients
3 cups bread flour
1 tablespoon yeast
   (2¼ teaspoons for bread
   machines)
1 teaspoon salt
1 tablespoon sugar
1 teaspoon each cumin,
   oregano, black pepper,
   onion, garlic, dried and
   ground

Wet ingredients for batter bread
1½ cups water
1 tablespoon Worcestershire
   sauce
2 teaspoons liquid cayenne
   pepper
1 tablespoon tomato paste
1 egg, beaten

Wet ingredients for kneaded bread
⅔ cup water
1 tablespoon Worcestershire
   sauce
2 teaspoons liquid cayenne
   pepper

1 tablespoon tomato paste
1 egg, beaten

Wet ingredients for bread machines
1 cup water
1 tablespoon Worcestershire
   sauce
2 teaspoons liquid cayenne
   pepper
1 tablespoon tomato paste
1 egg, beaten

Steps for batter bread
Mix
1st rise
Stir down, 2nd rise
Bake at 375° for 50 minutes
Test for doneness and cool

Steps for kneaded bread
Mix, knead, oil bowl
1st rise
Punch down, 2nd rise
Shape into loaf, 3rd rise
Crust: soft
Bake at 400° for 25 minutes
Test for doneness and cool

Crust: soft
Brush loaf with milk *before* baking.
   Or
Brush loaf with melted butter *after* baking.

Hot and Spicy Mustard Bread with Dill

Dry ingredients
3 cups bread flour
1 tablespoon yeast
  (2¼ teaspoons for bread
  machines)
1 teaspoon salt
1 tablespoon sugar
3 tablespoons dill weed, dried

**Wet ingredients for
batter bread**
1¾ cups water
3½ tablespoons hot and spicy
  mustard

**Wet ingredients for
kneaded bread**
1 cup water
3½ tablespoons hot and spicy
  mustard

**Wet ingredients for
bread machines**
1⅛ cups water
3½ tablespoons hot and spicy
  mustard

Steps for batter bread
Mix
1st rise
Stir down, 2nd rise
Bake at 375° for 50 minutes
Test for doneness and cool

Steps for kneaded bread
Mix, knead, oil bowl
1st rise
Punch down, 2nd rise
Shape into a loaf, 3rd rise
Crust: very chewy
Bake at 400° for 25 minutes
Test for doneness and cool

Crust: very chewy
Prepare egg wash: Mix 1 beaten egg with 1
tablespoon milk or water. Before baking, brush
with egg wash. Then steam: Place a pan on the
floor of the oven. Preheat oven to full heat. Toss
6 to 8 ice cubes into the pan, place the loaf in
right away, and close the door quickly.

VEGGIE BREADS
Six-Veggies Bread

Dry ingredients
3 cups bread flour
1 tablespoon yeast
   (2¼ teaspoons for bread
   machines)
1 teaspoon salt
1 tablespoon sugar
2 tablespoons carrot, grated
1 tablespoon each red bell
   pepper, green bell pepper,
   mushrooms, and celery,
   diced very small
½ cup red onion, diced
   very small

**Wet ingredients for
batter bread**
1¾ cups water
1 tablespoon olive oil

**Wet ingredients for
kneaded bread**
1 cup water
1 tablespoon olive oil

**Wet ingredients for
bread machines**
1 cup + 2 tablespoons water
1 tablespoon olive oil

Steps for batter bread
Mix
1st rise
Stir down, 2nd rise
Bake at 375° for 50 minutes
Test for doneness and cool

Steps for kneaded bread
Mix, knead, oil bowl
1st rise
Punch down, 2nd rise
Shape into a loaf, 3rd rise
Crust: soft
Bake at 400° for 25 minutes
Test for doneness and cool

Crust: soft
Brush loaf with milk *before* baking.
   Or
Brush loaf with melted butter *after* baking.

Red Bell Pepper Bread with Cumin Seeds

Dry ingredients
3 cups bread flour
1 tablespoon yeast
(2¼ teaspoons for bread machines)
1 teaspoon salt
1 tablespoon sugar
1½ tablespoons cumin seeds
1 cup red bell pepper, diced small

Wet ingredients for batter bread
1¾ cups milk
1 tablespoon olive oil

Wet ingredients for kneaded bread
1 cup milk
1 tablespoon olive oil

Wet ingredients for bread machines
1 cup + 2 tablespoons milk
1 tablespoon olive oil

Steps for batter bread
Mix
1st rise
Stir down, 2nd rise
Bake at 350° for 50 minutes
Test for doneness and cool

Steps for kneaded bread
Mix, knead, oil bowl
1st rise
Punch down, 2nd rise
Shape into a loaf, 3rd rise
Crust: cumin seeds
Bake at 400° for 25 minutes
Test for doneness and cool

Crust: topping of cumin seeds
Prepare egg wash: Mix 1 beaten egg with 1 tablespoon milk or water. Before baking, brush with egg wash, sprinkle with topping, and brush with egg wash again, using a patting motion.

Green Olive Bread

Dry ingredients
3 cups bread flour
1 tablespoon yeast
  ($2\frac{1}{4}$ teaspoons for bread
  machines)
1 teaspoon salt
1 tablespoon sugar
$\frac{2}{3}$ cup green olives with
  pimientos, chopped small

**Wet ingredients for
batter bread**
$1\frac{3}{4}$ cups water
1 tablespoon olive oil

**Wet ingredients for
kneaded bread**
1 cup water
1 tablespoon olive oil

**Wet ingredients for
bread machines**
1 cup + 2 tablespoons water
1 tablespoon olive oil

Steps for batter bread
Mix
1st rise
Stir down, 2nd rise
Bake at $350°$ for 55 minutes
Test for doneness and cool

Steps for kneaded bread
Mix, knead, oil bowl
1st rise
Punch down, 2nd rise
Shape into a loaf, 3rd rise
Crust: chewy
Bake $400°$ for 25 minutes
Test for doneness and cool

Crust: chewy
Steam the loaf: Place a pan on the floor of
the oven. Preheat oven to full heat. Toss 6
to 8 ice cubes into the pan, place the loaf in
right away, and close the door quickly.

Red Bread

Dry ingredients
3 cups bread flour
1 tablespoon yeast
  ($2\frac{1}{4}$ teaspoons for bread
  machines)
1 teaspoon salt
1 tablespoon sugar
1 15-ounce can shredded beets
  (drain well and save liquid)

Wet ingredients for batter bread
1 cup beet juice
$\frac{1}{2}$ cup water
1 tablespoon melted butter

Wet ingredients for kneaded bread
1 cup beet juice
1 tablespoon melted butter

Wet ingredients for bread machines
1 cup + 2 tablespoons beet
  juice
1 tablespoon melted butter

Steps for batter bread
Mix
1st rise
Stir down, 2nd rise
Bake 350° for 50 minutes
Test for doneness and cool

Steps for kneaded bread
Mix, knead, oil bowl
1st rise
Punch down, 2nd rise
Shape into a loaf, 3rd rise
Crust: chewy
Bake at 400° for 30 minutes
Test for doneness and cool

Note: If there is not enough beet juice, add water to make up the difference called for in the recipe.

Crust: chewy
Steam the loaf: Place a pan on the floor of the oven. Preheat oven to full heat. Toss 6 to 8 ice cubes into the pan, place the loaf in right away, and close the door quickly.

Veggie Bread Variations

Based on "Red Bread" recipe. Omit beets and beet juice; add one of the following to the wet ingredients.

Bread	Batter breads	Kneaded breads	Bread machines
Spinach bread	1 15-ounce can chopped spinach with liquid + ½ cup water —or 2 cups fresh spinach, chopped small and packed, cooked in 1¾ cups water. Use all the liquid.	1 15-ounce can chopped spinach with liquid —or 2 cups fresh spinach, chopped small and packed, cooked in 1½ cups water. Use 1 cup of the liquid.	1 15-ounce can chopped spinach with liquid + ⅛ cup water —or 2 cups fresh spinach, chopped small and packed, cooked in 1½ cups water. Use 1 cup + 2 tablespoons of the liquid.
Carrot bread	2 cups carrots, grated and cooked in 1¾ cups water. Puree in the liquid and use all.	2 cups carrots, grated and cooked in 1½ cups water. Puree in the liquid and use all.	2 cups carrots, grated and cooked in 1¼ cups water. Puree in the liquid and use all.
Tomato paste bread	1 6-ounce can tomato paste mixed with 1¾ cups water. Use all the liquid.	1 6-ounce can tomato paste mixed with 1¼ cups water. Use all the liquid.	1 6-ounce can tomato paste mixed with 1½ cups water. Use all the liquid.

IV
White Breads with Cheese and Meat

The flavor of these breads is hard to beat. Read all labels for non-fat cheeses. Some manufacturers do not recommend cooking with them; however, I use all low-fat cheeses and have never had a problem.

When making breads with meat, cheese, or other added dry ingredients, it is best to mix the additions with the flour, before adding any wet ingredients. You can experiment with creating your own combinations for these breads. Be sure that the additions don't increase the amount of liquid significantly. Meats should be cooked thoroughly, drained, and dried on a paper towel. Raw ingredients such as green onions should be drained on a towel after they are rinsed.

See Chapter XI (under "Focaccia" and "Pizza"), for breads with meat and cheese toppings.

CHEESE BREADS
Cheddar Herb Bread

Dry ingredients
3 cups bread flour
1 tablespoon yeast
(2¼ teaspoons for bread
machines)
1 teaspoon salt
1 tablespoon sugar
3 tablespoons each fresh
oregano, basil, parsley,
cilantro, and sage,
chopped small
1 tablespoon garlic, minced
(optional)
1 cup cheddar cheese,
shredded

**Wet ingredients for
batter bread**
1¾ cups water
1 tablespoon olive oil

**Wet ingredients for
kneaded bread**
1 cup water
1 tablespoon olive oil

**Wet ingredients for
bread machines**
1⅛–1¼ cups water as required
1 tablespoon olive oil

Steps for batter bread
Mix
1st rise
Stir down, 2nd rise
Bake at 375° for 50 minutes
Test for doneness and cool

Steps for kneaded bread
Mix, knead, oil bowl
1st rise
Punch down, 2nd rise
Shape into loaf, 3rd rise
Crust: cheddar cheese
Bake at 375° for 30 minutes
Test for doneness and cool

Crust: topping of cheddar cheese
Sprinkle with shredded cheddar cheese
before the last 10 minutes of baking.

Cheddar, Cilantro, Onion Bread with Sun-Dried Tomatoes

Dry ingredients
3 cups bread flour
1 tablespoon yeast
  (2¼ teaspoons for bread
  machines)
1 teaspoon salt
1 tablespoon sugar
½ cup fresh cilantro, chopped
  small and packed
½ cup red onion, diced small
1 cup sun-dried tomatoes, diced
  very small and loosely packed
1 cup sharp cheddar cheese,
  shredded

**Wet ingredients for
batter bread**
1½ cups water
¼ cup sour cream
1 egg, beaten

**Wet ingredients for
kneaded bread**
¾ cup water
¼ cup sour cream
1 egg, beaten

**Wet ingredients for
bread machines**
1 cup water
¼ cup sour cream
1 egg, beaten

Steps for batter bread
Mix
1st rise
Stir down, 2nd rise
Bake at 375° for 50 minutes
Test for doneness and cool

Steps for kneaded bread
Mix, knead, oil bowl
1st rise
Punch down, 2nd rise
Shape into loaf, 3rd rise
Crust: chewy
Bake at 375° for 30–35
  minutes
Test for doneness and cool

Crust: chewy
Steam the loaf: Place a pan on the floor of
the oven. Preheat oven to full heat. Toss 6
to 8 ice cubes into the pan, place the loaf in
right away, and close the door quickly.

Cheese and Jalapeño Bread

Dry ingredients
2½ cups bread flour
1 tablespoon yeast
(2¼ teaspoons for bread
machines)
1 teaspoon salt
1 tablespoon sugar
¼ teaspoon baking soda
¾ cup cheddar cheese,
shredded
¼ cup green chiles (mild or
hot), seeded and diced
very small

Wet ingredients for batter bread
¾ cup water
1 cup buttermilk
1 egg, beaten
½ cup cream style corn

Wet ingredients for kneaded bread
2 tablespoons water
⅔ cup buttermilk
1 egg, beaten
½ cup cream style corn

Wet ingredients for bread machines
2 tablespoons water
1 cup buttermilk
1 egg, beaten
½ cup cream-style corn

Steps for batter bread
Mix
1st rise
Stir down, 2nd rise
Bake at 375° for 50–55
minutes
Test for doneness and cool

Steps for kneaded bread
Mix, knead, oil bowl
1st rise
Punch down, 2nd rise
Shape into loaf, 3rd rise
Crust: soft
Bake at 375° for 30 minutes
Test for doneness and cool

Crust: soft
Brush loaf with milk *before* baking.
  Or
Brush loaf with melted butter *after* baking.

Chile Cheese Jalapeño Bread

Dry ingredients
3 cups bread flour
1 tablespoon yeast
  (2¼ teaspoons for bread
  machines)
1 teaspoon salt
1 tablespoon sugar
½ cup jalapeño or mild chiles,
  seeded and diced small
1 tablespoon chile powder
1 teaspoon cumin, ground
1 cup jalapeño cheese,
  shredded
½ cup red onion, diced small

Wet ingredients for batter bread
1¾ cups water
1 tablespoon olive oil or hot
  chile oil
1 tablespoon tomato paste

Wet ingredients for kneaded bread
1 cup water
1 tablespoon olive oil or hot
  chile oil
1 tablespoon tomato paste

Wet ingredients for bread machines
1⅛–1¼ cups water as required
1 tablespoon olive oil or hot
  chile oil
1 tablespoon tomato paste

Steps for batter bread
Mix
1st rise
Stir down, 2nd rise
Bake at 375° for 50 minutes
Test for doneness and cool

Steps for kneaded bread
Mix, knead, oil bowl
1st rise
Punch down, 2nd rise
Shape into loaf, 3rd rise
Crust: chewy
Bake at 375° for 30 minutes
Test for doneness and cool

Crust: chewy
Steam the loaf: Place a pan on the floor of
the oven. Preheat oven to full heat. Toss 6
to 8 ice cubes into the pan, place the loaf in
right away, and close the door quickly.

Pepper Cheese, and Frito Chili Bread

Dry ingredients
2 cups bread flour
1 cup chili cheese corn chips,
  crumbled very small
1 tablespoon yeast
  (2¼ teaspoons for bread
  machines)
1 tablespoon sugar
1 cup pepper cheese or
  jalapeño cheese, shredded
½ cup green onions, thinly
  sliced

Wet ingredients for batter bread
1¾ cups water

Wet ingredients for kneaded bread
1 cup + 3 tablespoons water

Wet ingredients for bread machines
1⅛–1¼ cups water as required

Steps for batter breads
Mix
1st rise
Stir down, 2nd rise
Bake at 375⁰ for 50 minutes
Test for doneness and cool

Steps for kneaded bread
Mix, knead, oil bowl
1st rise
Punch down, 2nd rise
Shape into loaf, 3rd rise
Crust: chewy
Bake at 375⁰ for 30 minutes
Test for doneness and cool

Crust: chewy
Steam the loaf: Place a pan on the floor of the oven. Preheat oven to full heat. Toss 6 to 8 ice cubes into the pan, place the loaf in right away, and close the door quickly.

Celery Seed Cheese Bread

Dry ingredients
3 cups bread flour
1 tablespoon yeast
   ($2\frac{1}{4}$ teaspoons for bread
   machines)
1 teaspoon salt
1 tablespoon sugar
$\frac{1}{2}$ cup celery leaves,
   chopped small
1 tablespoon celery seeds
1 cup mozzarella cheese,
   shredded

**Wet ingredients for
batter bread**
$1\frac{3}{4}$ cups water
2 teaspoons sesame seed oil

**Wet ingredients for
kneaded bread**
1 cup water
2 teaspoons sesame seed oil

**Wet ingredients for
bread machines**
1 cup + 2 tablespoons water
2 teaspoons sesame seed oil

Steps for batter bread
Mix
1st rise
Stir down, 2nd rise
Bake at 375^0 for 50 minutes
Test for doneness and cool

Steps for kneaded bread
Mix, knead, oil bowl
1st rise
Punch down, 2nd rise
Shape into loaf, 3rd rise
Crust: sesame seeds
Bake at 375^0 for 30 minutes
Test for doneness and cool

Crust: topping of sesame seeds
Prepare egg wash: Mix 1 beaten egg with
1 tablespoon milk or water. Before baking,
brush with egg wash, sprinkle with topping,
and brush with egg wash again, using a
patting motion.

Good Old Mustard and Mozzarella Bread

Dry ingredients
3 cups bread flour
1 tablespoon yeast
(2¼ teaspoons for bread
machines)
1 teaspoon salt
1 tablespoon sugar
1 cup mozzarella cheese,
shredded

**Wet ingredients for
batter bread**
1½ cups water
¼ cup mustard

**Wet ingredients for
kneaded bread**
¾ cup water
¼ cup mustard

**Wet ingredients for
bread machine**
1 cup water
¼ cup mustard

Steps for batter bread
Mix
1st rise
Stir down, 2nd rise
Bake at 375° for 50 minutes
Test for doneness and cool

Steps for kneaded bread
Mix, knead, oil bowl
1st rise
Punch down, 2nd rise
Shape into loaf, 3rd rise
Crust: very chewy
Bake at 375° for 30 minutes
Test for doneness and cool

Crust: very chewy
Prepare egg wash: Mix 1 beaten egg with 1
tablespoon milk or water. Before baking, brush
with egg wash. Then steam: Place a pan on the
floor of the oven. Preheat oven to full heat. Toss
6 to 8 ice cubes into the pan, place the loaf in
right away, and close the door quickly.

Provolone Cilantro Bread

Dry ingredients
3 cups bread flour
1 tablespoon yeast
  (2¼ teaspoons for bread
  machines)
1 teaspoon salt
1 tablespoon sugar
½ cup fresh cilantro, chopped
  small and packed
1 cup provolone cheese,
  shredded

**Wet ingredients for
batter bread**
1½ cups water
¼ cup sour cream

**Wet ingredients for
kneaded bread**
¾ cup water
¼ cup sour cream

**Wet ingredients for
bread machines**
1 cup water
¼ cup sour cream

Steps for batter bread
Mix
1st rise
Stir down, 2nd rise
Bake at 375° for 50 minutes
Test for doneness and cool

Steps for kneaded bread
Mix, knead, oil bowl
1st rise
Punch down, 2nd rise
Shape into loaf, 3rd rise
Crust: chewy
Bake at 375° for 30 minutes
Test for doneness and cool

Crust: chewy
Steam the loaf: Place a pan on the floor of
the oven. Preheat oven to full heat. Toss 6
to 8 ice cubes into the pan, place the loaf in
right away, and close the door quickly.

Muenster Dill Bread

Dry ingredients
3 cups bread flour
1 tablespoon yeast
(2¼ teaspoons for bread
machines)
1 teaspoon salt
1 tablespoon sugar
3 tablespoons dill weed, dried
1 cup Muenster cheese,
shredded

Wet ingredients for
batter bread
1 cup milk
¾ cup water
1 tablespoon olive oil

Wet ingredients for
kneaded bread
½ cup milk
½ cup water
1 tablespoon olive oil

Wet ingredients for
bread machines
¾ cup milk
⅛ cup water
1 tablespoon olive oil

Steps for batter bread
Mix
1st rise
Stir down, 2nd rise
Bake at 375° for 50–55
   minutes
Test for doneness and cool

Steps for kneaded bread
Mix, knead, oil bowl
1st rise
Punch down, 2nd rise
Shape into loaf, 3rd rise
Crust: dill weed
Bake at 375° for 30–35
   minutes
Test for doneness and cool

Crust: topping of dill weed
Prepare egg wash: Mix 1 beaten egg with 1
tablespoon milk or water. Before baking, brush
with egg wash and sprinkle with topping.

Muenster Bread with Rosemary and Green Onions

Dry ingredients
3 cups bread flour
1 tablespoon yeast
(2¼ teaspoons for bread machines)
1 teaspoon salt
1 tablespoon sugar
¼ cup fresh rosemary, chopped small
½ cup green onion tops, thinly sliced
1 cup Muenster cheese, shredded

Wet ingredients for batter bread
1¾ cups water
1 tablespoon olive oil

Wet ingredients for kneaded bread
1 cup water
1 tablespoon olive oil

Wet ingredients for bread machines
1 cup + 2 tablespoons water
1 tablespoon olive oil

Steps for batter bread
Mix
1st rise
Stir down, 2nd rise
Bake at 375° for 50 minutes
Test for doneness and cool

Steps for kneaded bread
Mix, knead, oil bowl
1st rise
Punch down, 2nd rise
Shape into loaf, 3rd rise
Crust: rosemary
Bake at 375° for 30 minutes
Test for doneness and cool

Crust: topping of fresh rosemary, chopped
Prepare egg wash: Mix 1 beaten egg with 1 tablespoon milk or water. Before baking, brush with egg wash, sprinkle with topping, and brush with egg wash again, using a patting motion.

Port Wine Cheese Bread with Onion

Note: Mix the port wine cheese spread with the wet ingredients until smooth; then bring to temperature (120°).

Dry ingredients
3 cups bread flour
1 tablespoon yeast
  (2¼ teaspoons for bread
  machines)
1 teaspoon salt
1 tablespoon sugar
½ cup red onion, diced small

Wet ingredients for batter bread
1¾ cups milk
1 tablespoon olive oil
1 cup port wine cheese spread

Wet ingredients for kneaded bread
1 cup milk
1 tablespoon olive oil
1 cup port wine cheese spread

Wet ingredients for bread machines
1 cup + 2 tablespoons milk
1 tablespoon olive oil
1 cup port wine cheese spread

Steps for batter bread
Mix
1st rise
Stir down, 2nd rise
Bake at 375° for 50–55
  minutes
Test for doneness and cool

Steps for kneaded bread
Mix, knead, oil bowl
1st rise
Punch down, 2nd rise
Shape into loaf, 3rd rise
Crust: soft
Bake at 375° for 30 minutes
Test for doneness and cool

Crust: soft
Brush loaf with milk *before* baking.
  Or
Brush loaf with melted butter *after* baking.

Mustard and Swiss Cheese Bread

Dry ingredients
3 cups bread flour
1 tablespoon yeast
   (2¼ teaspoons for bread
   machines)
1 teaspoon salt
1 tablespoon sugar
3 tablespoons caraway seeds
¼ teaspoon garlic powder
1 cup Swiss cheese, shredded

**Wet ingredients for
batter bread**
1½ cups water
¼ cup mustard
1 egg, beaten

**Wet ingredients for
kneaded bread**
¾ cup water
¼ cup mustard
1 egg, beaten

**Wet ingredients for
bread machines**
1 cup water
¼ cup mustard
1 egg, beaten

Steps for batter bread
Mix
1st rise
Stir down, 2nd rise
Bake at 375° for 50 minutes
Test for doneness and cool

Steps for kneaded bread
Mix, knead, oil bowl
1st rise
Punch down, 2nd rise
Shape into loaf, 3rd rise
Crust: caraway seeds
Bake at 375° for 30 minutes
Test for doneness and cool

Variation: Shape round (p. 21).
Crust, caraway seeds (as above)

Crust: topping of caraway seeds
Prepare egg wash: Mix 1 beaten egg with
1 tablespoon milk or water. Before baking,
brush with egg wash, sprinkle with topping,
and brush with egg wash again, using a
patting motion.

Cheesy Spinach and Pine Nut Bread

Dry ingredients
3 cups bread flour
1 tablespoon yeast
(2¼ teaspoons for bread
machines)
1 teaspoon salt
1 tablespoon sugar
½ cup pine nuts, coarsely
chopped
1 cup Colby cheese, shredded

**Wet ingredients for
batter bread**
1¾ cups water
1 tablespoon olive oil
1 cup fresh spinach, chopped
small and packed

**Wet ingredients for
kneaded bread**
1 cup water
1 tablespoon olive oil
1 cup fresh spinach, chopped
small and packed

Variation: Substitute one 10-
ounce package frozen
chopped spinach, defrosted
with the moisture squeezed
out; or same amount of
fresh or frozen broccoli, cau-
liflower, kale, or mustard
greens.

**Wet ingredients for
bread machines**
1⅛–1¼ cups water as required
1 tablespoon olive oil
1 cup fresh spinach, chopped
small and packed

Steps for batter bread
Mix
1st rise
Stir down, 2nd rise
Bake at 375° for 50 minutes
Test for doneness and cool

Steps for kneaded bread
Mix, knead, oil bowl
1st rise
Punch down, 2nd rise
Shape into loaf, 3rd rise
Crust: pine nuts
Bake at 375° for 30 minutes
Test for doneness and cool

**Crust: topping of pine nuts,
chopped small**
Prepare egg wash: Mix 1
beaten egg with 1 table-
spoon milk or water. Before
baking, brush with egg
wash, sprinkle with top-
ping, and brush with egg
wash again, using a patting
motion.

Smoked Cheese with Onion and Garlic Bread

Dry ingredients
3 cups bread flour
1 tablespoon yeast
 (2¼ teaspoons for bread
 machines)
1 teaspoon salt
1 tablespoon sugar
½ cup red onion, diced small
1 tablespoon garlic, minced,
 sauteed, and drained
1 cup smoked cheese,
 shredded (your choice)

**Wet ingredients for
batter bread**
1 cup water
¾ cup milk

**Wet ingredients for
kneaded bread**
½ cup water
½ cup milk

**Wet ingredients for
bread machines**
¾ cup water
½ cup milk

Steps for batter bread
Mix
1st rise
Stir down, 2nd rise
Bake at 375° for 50–55
 minutes
Test for doneness and cool

Steps for kneaded bread
Mix, knead, oil bowl
1st rise
Punch down, 2nd rise
Shape into loaf, 3rd rise
Crust: soft
Bake at 400° for 25 minutes
Test for doneness and cool

Crust: soft
Brush loaf with milk *before* baking.
 Or
Brush loaf with melted butter *after* baking.

Buttermilk Cheese Bread

Dry ingredients
3 cups bread flour
1 tablespoon yeast
  (2¼ teaspoons for bread
  machines)
1 teaspoon salt
1 tablespoon sugar
¼ teaspoon baking soda
1 cup American cheese,
  shredded

**Wet ingredients for
batter bread**
1½ cups buttermilk
1 egg, beaten

**Wet ingredients for
kneaded bread**
¾ cup buttermilk
1 egg, beaten

**Wet ingredients for
bread machines**
1 cup buttermilk
1 egg, beaten

Steps for batter bread
Mix
1st rise
Stir down, 2nd rise
Bake at 375° for 50 minutes
Test for doneness and cool

Steps for kneaded bread
Mix, knead, oil bowl
1st rise
Punch down, 2nd rise
Shape into loaf, 3rd rise
Crust: soft
Bake at 375° for 30 minutes
Test for doneness and cool

Crust: soft
Brush loaf with milk *before* baking.
  Or
Brush loaf with melted butter *after* baking.

Bell Pepper Cheese Bread

Dry ingredients
3 cups bread flour
1 tablespoon yeast
  ($2\frac{1}{4}$ teaspoons for bread
  machines)
1 teaspoon salt
1 tablespoon sugar
$\frac{1}{4}$ cup each red, yellow, and
  green bell pepper, diced small
1 tablespoon garlic, minced
1 cup American cheese,
  shredded

**Wet ingredients for
batter bread**
$1\frac{3}{4}$ cups water
1 tablespoon olive oil

**Wet ingredients for
kneaded bread**
1 cup water
1 tablespoon olive oil

**Wet ingredients for
bread machines**
1 cup + 2 tablespoons water
1 tablespoon olive oil

Steps for batter bread
Mix
1st rise
Stir down, 2nd rise
Bake at 375^0 for 50–55
  minutes
Test for doneness and cool

Steps for kneaded bread
Mix, knead, oil bowl
1st rise
Punch down, 2nd rise
Shape into loaf, 3rd rise
Crust: soft
Bake at 375^0 for 30 minutes
Test for doneness and cool

Crust: soft
Brush loaf with milk *before* baking.
  Or
Brush loaf with melted butter *after* baking.

Carrot Zucchini Cheese Bread

Dry ingredients
3 cups bread flour
1 tablespoon yeast
   (2¼ teaspoons for bread
   machines)
1 teaspoon salt
1 tablespoon sugar
½ cup zucchini, shredded and
   blotted with paper towel
½ cup carrots, shredded
¼ cup toasted sunflower seeds,
   coarsely chopped
1 cup American cheese,
   shredded

**Wet ingredients for
batter bread**
1¾ cups water
1 egg, beaten

**Wet ingredients for
kneaded bread**
1 cup water
1 egg, beaten

**Wet ingredients for
bread machines**
1 cup + 2 tablespoons water
1 egg, beaten

Steps for batter bread
Mix
1st rise
Stir down, 2nd rise
Bake at 375° for 50–55
   minutes
Test for doneness and cool

Steps for kneaded bread
Mix, knead, oil bowl
1st rise
Punch down, 2nd rise
Shape into loaf, 3rd rise
Crust: sunflower seeds
Bake at 350° for 30–35
   minutes
Test for doneness and cool

Crust: topping of sunflower seeds
Prepare egg wash: Mix 1 beaten egg with
1 tablespoon milk or water. Before baking,
brush with egg wash, sprinkle with topping,
and brush with egg wash again, using a
patting motion.

Italian Easter Bread

Dry ingredients
3 cups bread flour
1 tablespoon yeast
 (2¼ teaspoons for bread
 machines)
1 tablespoon sugar
1 cup fresh Parmesan cheese,
 grated
1 teaspoon black pepper,
 ground, or to taste

**Wet ingredients for
batter bread**
1 cup milk
¼ cup melted butter
2 eggs, beaten
2 tablespoons olive oil

**Wet ingredients for
kneaded bread**
½ cup milk
¼ cup melted butter
2 eggs, beaten
2 tablespoons olive oil

**Wet ingredients for
bread machines**
½ cup + 2 tablespoons milk
¼ cup melted butter
2 eggs, beaten
2 tablespoons olive oil

Steps for batter bread
Mix
1st rise
Stir down, 2nd rise
Bake at 375° for 50 minutes
Test for doneness and cool

Steps for kneaded bread
Mix, knead, oil bowl
1st rise
Punch down, 2nd rise
Shape into loaf, 3rd rise
Crust: soft
Bake at 375° for 30 minutes
Test for doneness and cool

Crust: soft
Brush loaf with milk *before* baking.
 Or
Brush loaf with melted butter *after* baking.

Parmesan Pesto Bread

Dry ingredients
3 cups bread flour
1 tablespoon yeast
(2¼ teaspoons for bread
machines)
1 teaspoon salt
1 tablespoon sugar
1/2 cup fresh Parmesan
cheese, shredded

**Wet ingredients for
batter bread**
1¾ cups water
½ cup pesto sauce (your
choice)

**Wet ingredients for
kneaded bread**
¾ cup water
½ cup pesto sauce

**Wet ingredients for
bread machines**
1 cup water
½ cup pesto sauce

Steps for batter bread
Mix
1st rise
Stir down, 2nd rise
Bake at 375° for 50 minutes
Test for doneness and cool

Steps for kneaded bread
Mix, knead, oil bowl
1st rise
Punch down, 2nd rise
Shape into loaf, 3rd rise
Crust: Parmesan cheese (p. 22)
Bake at 400° for 25 minutes
Test for doneness and cool

Crust: topping of Parmesan cheese
Prepare egg wash: Mix 1 beaten egg with 1
tablespoon milk or water. Before baking, brush
with egg wash and sprinkle with topping.

Parmesan Garlic Bread with Shallots and Basil

Dry ingredients
3 cups bread flour
1 tablespoon yeast
  (2¼ teaspoons for bread
  machines)
1 teaspoon salt
1 tablespoon sugar
½ cup fresh Parmesan cheese,
  shredded
⅔ cup fresh basil, chopped
  small and loosely packed
1 tablespoon garlic or to taste
¼ cup shallots, diced small and
  packed

Wet ingredients for batter bread
1¾ cups water
2 tablespoons olive oil

Wet ingredients for kneaded bread
1 cup water
2 tablespoons olive oil

Wet ingredients for bread machines
1⅛–1¼ cups water as required
2 tablespoons olive oil

Steps for batter bread
Mix
1st rise
Stir down, 2nd rise
Bake at 375° for 50 minutes
Test for doneness and cool

Steps for kneaded bread
Mix, knead, oil bowl
1st rise
Punch down, 2nd rise
Shape into loaf, 3rd rise
Crust: soft
Bake at 375° for 30 minutes
Test for doneness and cool

Crust: soft
Brush loaf with milk *before* baking.
  Or
Brush loaf with melted butter *after* baking.

Ricotta Cheese and Chives Bread

Dry ingredients
3 cups bread flour
1 tablespoon yeast
(2¼ teaspoons for bread
machines)
1 teaspoon salt
1 tablespoon sugar
½ cup green onions, thinly
sliced and packed

Wet ingredients for batter bread
1¼ cups milk
½ cup ricotta cheese, at room
temperature
2 eggs, beaten

Wet ingredients for kneaded bread
½ cup milk
½ cup ricotta cheese, at room
temperature
2 eggs, beaten

Wet ingredients for bread machines
¾ cup milk
½ cup ricotta cheese, at room
temperature
2 eggs, beaten

Steps for batter bread
Mix
1st rise
Stir down, 2nd rise
Bake at 375° for 50 minutes
Test for doneness and cool

Steps for kneaded bread
Mix, knead, oil bowl
1st rise
Punch down, 2nd rise
Shape into loaf, 3rd rise
Crust: soft
Bake at 375° degrees for 30
minutes
Test for doneness and cool

Crust: soft
Brush loaf with milk *before* baking.
  Or
Brush loaf with melted butter *after* baking.

Cottage Cheese Chive Bread

Dry ingredients
3 cups bread flour
1 tablespoon yeast
  (2¼ teaspoons for bread
  machines)
1 teaspoon salt
1 tablespoon sugar
1 cup green onions, thinly
  sliced

**Wet ingredients for
batter bread**
1¼ cups milk
½ cup cottage cheese, small
  curd
1 egg, beaten

**Wet ingredients for
kneaded bread**
½ cup milk
¼ cup cottage cheese
1 egg, beaten

**Wet ingredients for
bread machines**
1 cup milk
¼ cup cottage cheese
1 egg, beaten

Steps for batter bread
Mix
1st rise
Stir down, 2nd rise
Bake at 375° for 50 minutes
Test for doneness and cool

Steps for kneaded bread
Mix, knead, oil bowl
1st rise
Punch down, 2nd rise
Shape into loaf, 3rd rise
Crust: poppy seeds
Bake at 375° for 30 minutes
Test for doneness and cool

Crust: topping of poppy seeds
Prepare egg wash: Mix 1 beaten egg with
1 tablespoon milk or water. Before baking,
brush with egg wash, sprinkle with topping,
and brush with egg wash again, using a
patting motion.

MEAT AND CHEESE BREADS

Cheese and Sausage Bread

Dry ingredients
3 cups bread flour
1 tablespoon yeast
   (2¼ teaspoons for bread
   machines)
1 teaspoon salt
1 tablespoon sugar
1 cup sausage, ground, fried,
   and drained
1 cup smoked cheese,
   shredded

**Wet ingredients for
batter bread**
1¾ cups water
1 tablespoon oil (optional)

**Wet ingredients for
kneaded bread**
1 cup water
1 tablespoon oil (optional)

**Wet ingredients for
bread machines**
1⅛–1¼ cups water as required
1 tablespoon oil (optional)

Steps for batter bread
Mix
1st rise
Stir down
Bake at 375⁰ for 50 minutes
Test for doneness and cool

Steps for kneaded bread
Mix, knead, oil bowl
1st rise
Punch down, 2nd rise
Shape into a loaf, 3rd rise
Crust: soft
Bake at 400⁰ for 25–30
   minutes
Test for doneness and cool

Crust: soft
Brush loaf with milk *before* baking.
   Or
Brush loaf with melted butter *after* baking.

Chili Jalapeño Bread

Dry ingredients
3 cups bread flour
1 tablespoon yeast
  (2¼ teaspoons for bread
  machines)
1 teaspoon salt
1 tablespoon sugar
1 cup chili, mashed
1 cup jalapeño cheese,
  shredded

**Wet ingredients for
batter bread**
1½ cups water
1 tablespoon oil (optional)

**Wet ingredients for
kneaded bread**
1 cup water
1 tablespoon oil (optional)

**Wet ingredients for
bread machines**
1⅛–1¼ cups water as required
1 tablespoon oil (optional)

Steps for batter bread
Mix
1st rise
Stir down
Bake at 375° for 50 minutes
Test for doneness and cool

Steps for kneaded bread
Mix, knead, oil bowl
1st rise
Punch down, 2nd rise
Shape into a loaf, 3rd rise
Crust: soft
Bake at 400° for 25–30
  minutes
Test for doneness and cool

Crust: soft
Brush loaf with milk *before* baking.
  Or
Brush loaf with melted butter *after* baking.

Pizza Bread

Dry ingredients
3 cups bread flour
1 tablespoon yeast
   (2¼ teaspoons for bread
   machines)
1 teaspoon salt
1 tablespoon sugar
1 cup pepperoni, diced small,
   fried, and drained
¼ cup each green bell pepper
   and onion, diced small
1 cup mozzarella cheese,
   shredded

Wet ingredients for
batter bread
1¼ cups water
1 tablespoon oil (optional)
½ cup + 3 tablespoons
   pizza sauce

Wet ingredients for
kneaded bread
1 cup water
1 tablespoon oil (optional)

Wet ingredients for
bread machine
1⅛–1¼ cups water as required
1 tablespoon oil (optional)

Steps for batter bread
Mix
1st rise
Stir down
Bake at 375° for 50 minutes
Test for doneness and cool

Steps for kneaded bread
Mix, knead, oil bowl
1st rise
Punch down, 2nd rise
Shape into a loaf, 3rd rise
Crust: soft
Bake at 400° for 25–30
   minutes
Test for doneness and cool

Crust: soft
Brush loaf with milk *before* baking.
   Or
Brush loaf with melted butter *after* baking.

Savory Chicken and Cheese Bread

Dry ingredients
3 cups bread flour
1 tablespoon yeast
   (2¼ teaspoons for bread
   machines)
1 teaspoon salt
1 tablespoon sugar
1 cup cooked chicken,
   diced small
3 tablespoons each fresh basil,
   oregano, cilantro, and sage,
   chopped small and packed
1 cup mild cheddar cheese,
   shredded

**Wet ingredients for
batter bread**
1¾ cups water
1 tablespoon oil (optional)

**Wet ingredients for
kneaded bread**
1 cup water
1 tablespoon oil (optional)

**Wet ingredients for
bread machines**
1⅛–1¼ cups water as required
1 tablespoon oil (optional)

Steps for batter bread
Mix
1st rise
Stir down
Bake at 375° for 50 minutes
Test for doneness and cool

Steps for kneaded bread
Mix, knead, oil bowl
1st rise
Punch down, 2nd rise
Shape into a loaf, 3rd rise
Crust: soft
Bake at 400° for 25–30
   minutes
Test for doneness and cool

Crust: soft
Brush loaf with milk *before* baking.
   Or
Brush loaf with melted butter *after* baking.

Ham and Swiss Cheese Bread with Green Onions

Dry ingredients
3 cups bread flour
1 tablespoon yeast
  (2¼ teaspoons for bread machines)
1 teaspoon salt
1 tablespoon sugar
1 cup smoked ham, diced small
½ cup green onions, thinly sliced and packed
1 cup Swiss cheese, shredded

Wet ingredients for batter bread
1¾ cups water
1 tablespoon oil (optional)

Wet ingredients for kneaded bread
1 cup water
1 tablespoon oil (optional)

Wet ingredients for bread machines
1⅛–1¼ cups water as required
1 tablespoon oil (optional)

Steps for batter bread
Mix
1st rise
Stir down
Bake at 375° for 50 minutes
Test for doneness and cool

Steps for kneaded bread
Mix, knead, oil bowl
1st rise
Punch down, 2nd rise
Shape into a loaf, 3rd rise
Crust: soft
Bake at 400° for 25–30 minutes
Test for doneness and cool

Crust: soft
Brush loaf with milk *before* baking.
  Or
Brush loaf with melted butter *after* baking.

Peppery Italian Cheese Bread with Bacon

Dry ingredients
3 cups bread flour
1 tablespoon yeast
(2¼ teaspoons for bread machines)
1 teaspoon salt
1 tablespoon sugar
1 cup bacon, diced, fried, and drained
1 cup provolone cheese, shredded
½ cup fresh basil, chopped small and packed
2 teaspoons freshly ground pepper or to taste

Wet ingredients for batter bread
1¾ cups milk

Wet ingredients for kneaded bread
1 cup milk

Wet ingredients for bread machines
1 cup + 2 tablespoons milk

Steps for batter bread
Mix
1st rise
Stir down, 2nd rise
Bake at 375° for 50 minutes
Test for doneness and cool

Steps for kneaded bread
Mix, knead, oil bowl
1st rise
Punch down, 2nd rise
Shape into loaf, 3rd rise
Crust: pepper
Bake at 375° for 30–35 minutes
Test for doneness and cool

Variation: Substitute ½ cup finely chopped cilantro for basil.

Crust: topping of pepper
Prepare egg wash: Mix 1 beaten egg with 1 tablespoon milk or water. Before baking, brush with egg wash and sprinkle with topping.

Bacon and Cheese Bread with Cilantro

Dry ingredients
3 cups bread flour
1 tablespoon yeast
  (2¼ teaspoons for bread
  machines)
1 teaspoon salt
1 tablespoon sugar
1 cup bacon, diced, fried, and
  drained
¼ cup fresh cilantro, chopped
  small and packed
1 cup American cheese,
  shredded

**Wet ingredients for
batter bread**
1¾ cups water
1 tablespoon oil (optional)

**Wet ingredients for
kneaded bread**
1 cup water
1 tablespoon oil (optional)

**Wet ingredients for
bread machines**
1⅛–1¼ cups water as required
1 tablespoon oil (optional)

Steps for batter bread
Mix
1st rise
Stir down
Bake at 375° for 50 minutes
Test for doneness and cool

Steps for kneaded bread
Mix, knead, oil bowl
1st rise
Punch down, 2nd rise
Shape into a loaf, 3rd rise
Crust: soft
Bake at 400° for 25–30
  minutes
Test for doneness and cool

Crust: soft
Brush loaf with milk *before* baking.
  Or
Brush loaf with melted butter *after* baking.

V
Potato Breads

Potato breads are very flavorful. They have a nice soft crumb and make wonderful sandwiches. Most of these recipes call for **potato water,** made as follows:

You will need 1½ cups peeled and diced potatoes. Cover with 4 cups water and simmer until soft. Mash the potatoes in the same water they were cooked in, and let cool. This is your potato water. It can be refrigerated or frozen.

When you are in a hurry and have no potato water prepared, you can use instant potato flakes. GIVE AMOUNTS OF POTATO FLAKES AND WATER.

For those of you who would like to make the transition from store-bought soft white bread to homemade, this is a good bread to start with. The potato water keeps the bread moist and hastens rising. Your end product is a soft-textured bread that children really seem to like.

Quick Potato Bread

Dry ingredients
3 cups bread flour
1 tablespoon yeast
  (2 ¼ teaspoons for bread
  machines)
1 teaspoon salt
1 tablespoon sugar

Wet ingredients for batter bread
1 ¾ cups potato water
1 tablespoon olive oil

Wet ingredients for kneaded bread
1 cup potato water
1 tablespoon olive oil

Wet ingredients for bread machines
1 ⅛–1 ¼ cups potato water as
  required
1 tablespoon olive oil

Steps for batter bread
Mix
1st rise
Stir down, 2nd rise
Bake at 375° for 50 minutes
Test for doneness and cool

Steps for kneaded bread
Mix, knead, oil bowl
1st rise
Punch down
Shape into loaf, 2nd rise
Crust: soft
Bake at 400° for 25 minutes
Test for doneness and cool

Crust: soft
Brush loaf with milk *before* baking.
  Or
Brush loaf with melted butter *after* baking.

Potato Flour Bread

Dry ingredients
2 cups bread flour
1 tablespoon yeast
  (2¼ teaspoons for bread machines)
1 teaspoon salt
1 tablespoon sugar
1 cup potato flour (sold in health food stores)

Wet ingredients for batter bread
1¾ cups potato water
1 tablespoon olive oil

Wet ingredients for kneaded bread
1 cup potato water
1 tablespoon olive oil

Wet ingredients for bread machines
1⅛–1¼ cups potato water as required
1 tablespoon olive oil

Steps for batter bread
Mix
1st rise
Stir down, 2nd rise
Bake at 375° for 50 minutes
Test for doneness and cool

Steps for kneaded bread
Mix, knead, oil bowl
1st rise
Punch down, 2nd rise
Shape into loaf, 3rd rise
Crust: soft
Bake at 400° for 25 minutes
Test for doneness and cool

Crust: soft
Brush loaf with milk *before* baking.
  Or
Brush loaf with melted butter *after* baking.

Oatmeal Potato Bread

Dry ingredients
2 cups bread flour
1 cup oatmeal
1 tablespoon yeast
  (2¼ teaspoons for bread
  machines)
1 teaspoon salt
1 tablespoon brown sugar

**Wet ingredients for
batter bread**
1¾ cups potato water
1 tablespoon olive oil

**Wet ingredients for
kneaded bread**
1 cup potato water
1 tablespoon olive oil

**Wet ingredients for
bread machines**
1⅛–1¼ cups potato water as
  required
1 tablespoon olive oil

Steps for batter bread
Mix
1st rise
Stir down, 2nd rise
Bake at 375° for 50 minutes
Test for doneness and cool

Steps for kneaded bread
Mix, knead, oil bowl
1st rise
Punch down, 2nd rise
Shape into loaf, 3rd rise
Crust: soft
Bake at 400° for 25 minutes
Test for doneness and cool

Crust: soft
Brush loaf with milk *before* baking.
  Or
Brush loaf with melted butter *after* baking.

Potato Egg Bread

Dry ingredients
3 cups bread flour
1 tablespoon yeast
(2¼ teaspoons for bread
machines)
1 teaspoon salt
1 tablespoon sugar

Wet ingredients for batter bread
1½ cups potato water
2 eggs, beaten
1 tablespoon olive oil

Wet ingredients for kneaded bread
½ cup potato water
2 eggs, beaten
1 tablespoon olive oil

Wet ingredients for bread machines
1 cup potato water
2 eggs, beaten
1 tablespoon olive oil

Steps for batter bread
Mix
1st rise
Stir down, 2nd rise
Bake at 375° for 50 minutes
Test for doneness and cool

Steps for kneaded bread
Mix, knead, oil bowl
1st rise
Punch down, 2nd rise
Shape into loaf, 3rd rise
Crust: sesame seeds
Bake at 400° for 25 minutes
Test for doneness and cool

Crust: topping of sesame seeds
Prepare egg wash: Mix 1 beaten egg with
1 tablespoon milk or water. Before baking,
brush with egg wash, sprinkle with topping,
and brush with egg wash again, using a
patting motion.

Potato Onion Bread

Dry ingredients
3 cups bread flour
1 tablespoon yeast
(2¼ teaspoons for bread machines)
1 teaspoon salt
1 tablespoon sugar
3 tablespoons caraway seeds
1 cup onion, diced small, sauteed in 1½ tablespoons butter, and drained

Wet ingredients for batter bread
1¾ cups potato water
1 tablespoon olive oil

Wet ingredients for kneaded bread
1 cup potato water
1 tablespoon olive oil

Wet ingredients for bread machines
1⅛–1¼ cups potato water as required
1 tablespoon olive oil

Steps for batter bread
Mix
1st rise
Stir down, 2nd rise
Bake at 375° for 50 minutes
Test for doneness and cool

Steps for kneaded bread
Mix, knead, oil bowl
1st rise
Punch down, 2nd rise
Shape into loaf, 3nd rise
Crust: caraway seeds
Bake at 400° for 25 minutes
Test for doneness and cool

Crust: topping of caraway seeds
Prepare egg wash: Mix 1 beaten egg with 1 tablespoon milk or water. Before baking, brush with egg wash, sprinkle with topping, and brush with egg wash again, using a patting motion.

Potato, Carrot, and Millet Bread

Dry ingredients
2 cups bread flour
1 cup millet flour
(found in health food stores)
1 tablespoon yeast
(2¼ teaspoons for bread
machines)
1 teaspoon salt
1 tablespoon sugar
1½ cups carrots, grated

**Wet ingredients for
batter bread**
1¾ cups potato water
1 tablespoon olive oil

**Wet ingredients for
kneaded bread**
1 cup potato water
1 tablespoon olive oil

**Wet ingredients for
bread machines**
1⅛–1¼ cups potato water as
required
1 tablespoon olive oil

Steps for batter bread
Mix
1st rise
Stir down, 2nd rise
Bake at 375° for 50 minutes
Test for doneness and cool

Steps for kneaded bread
Mix, knead, oil bowl
1st rise
Punch down, 2nd rise
Shape into loaf, 3rd rise
Crust: chewy
Bake at 400° for 25 minutes
Test for doneness and cool

Crust: chewy
Steam the loaf: Place a pan on the floor of
the oven. Preheat oven to full heat. Toss 6
to 8 ice cubes into the pan, place the loaf in
right away, and close the door quickly.

Potato Bread with Sour Cream and Dill

Dry ingredients
3 cups bread flour
1 tablespoon yeast
  (2 ¼ teaspoons for bread
  machines)
1 teaspoon salt
1 tablespoon sugar
4 tablespoons dill weed, dried

**Wet ingredients for
batter bread**
1 cup potato water
¾ cup sour cream
1 tablespoon olive oil

**Wet ingredients for
kneaded bread**
½ cup potato water
½ cup sour cream
1 tablespoon olive oil

**Wet ingredients for
bread machines**
¾ cup potato water
½ cup sour cream
1 tablespoon olive oil

Steps for batter bread
Mix
1st rise
Stir down, 2nd rise
Bake at 375° for 50 minutes
Test for doneness and cool

Steps for kneaded bread
Mix, knead, oil bowl
1st rise
Punch down, 2nd rise
Shape into loaf, 3rd rise
Crust: dill weed
Bake at 400° for 25 minutes
Test for doneness and cool

Crust: topping of dill weed
Prepare egg wash: Mix 1 beaten egg with 1
tablespoon milk or water. Before baking, brush
with egg wash and sprinkle with topping.

Buttermilk Potato Bread with Fresh Rosemary

Dry ingredients
2 cups bread flour
1 cup oatmeal
1 tablespoon yeast
   ($2\frac{1}{4}$ teaspoons for bread machines)
1 teaspoon salt
1 tablespoon sugar
$\frac{1}{2}$ teaspoon baking soda
1 cup fresh rosemary, coarsely chopped and very loosely packed

Wet ingredients for batter bread
$1\frac{3}{4}$ cups potato water
1 cup buttermilk

Wet ingredients for kneaded bread
$\frac{1}{4}$ cup potato water
$\frac{3}{4}$ cup buttermilk

Wet ingredients for bread machines
$\frac{1}{4}$ cup potato water
$\frac{3}{4}$ cup + 2 tablespoons buttermilk

Steps for batter bread
Mix
1st rise
Stir down, 2nd rise
Bake at 375° for 50 minutes
Test for doneness and cool

Steps for kneaded bread
Mix, knead, oil bowl
1st rise
Punch down, 2nd rise
Shape into loaf, 3rd rise
Crust: soft
Bake at 400° for 25 minutes
Test for doneness and cool

Crust: soft
Brush loaf with milk *before* baking.
   Or
Brush loaf with melted butter *after* baking.

Onion and Broccoli Potato Bread

Dry ingredients
3 cups bread flour
1 tablespoon yeast
  (2¼ teaspoons for bread
  machines)
1 teaspoon salt
1 tablespoon sugar
1 cup fresh broccoli, chopped
  very small and cooked until
  just tender and drained well.
  Or 1 cup chopped frozen
  broccoli, defrosted and dried
  with a paper towel
1 cup red onion, diced small

Wet ingredients for batter bread
1¾ cups potato water
1 tablespoon olive oil

Wet ingredients for kneaded bread
1 cup potato water
1 tablespoon olive oil

Wet ingredients for bread machines
1⅛–1¼ cups potato water as
  required
1 tablespoon olive oil

Steps for batter bread
Mix
1st rise
Stir down, 2nd rise
Bake at 375° for 50 minutes
Test for doneness and cool

Steps for kneaded bread
Mix, knead, oil bowl
1st rise
Punch down, 2nd rise
Shape into loaf, 3rd rise
Crust: crisp
Bake at 400° for 25 minutes
Test for doneness and cool

Crust: crisp
Using a spray bottle, spray the loaf 4 times
with cold water during baking.

Fresh Sage, Thyme, and Onion Bread

Dry ingredients
3 cups bread flour
1 tablespoon yeast
(2 1/4 teaspoons for bread
machines)
1 teaspoon salt
1 tablespoon sugar
1/4 cup each fresh sage and
thyme, chopped small and
packed
1 cup red onion, diced small

**Wet ingredients for
batter bread**
1 3/4 cups potato water
1 tablespoon olive oil

**Wet ingredients for
kneaded bread**
1 cup potato water
1 tablespoon olive oil

**Wet ingredients for
bread machines**
1 1/8–1 1/4 cups potato water as
needed
1 tablespoon olive oil

Steps for batter bread
Mix
1st rise
Stir down, 2nd rise
Bake at 375° for 50 minutes
Test for doneness and cool

Steps for kneaded bread
Mix, knead, oil bowl
1st rise
Punch down, 2nd rise
Shape into loaf, 3rd rise
Crust: soft
Bake at 400° for 25 minutes
Test for doneness and cool

Crust: soft
Brush loaf with milk *before* baking.
  Or
Brush loaf with melted butter *after* baking.

Green Onion and Poppy Seed Potato Bread

Dry ingredients
3 cups bread flour
1 tablespoon yeast
  (2¼ teaspoons for bread
  machines)
1 teaspoon salt
1 tablespoon sugar
¾ cup green onion, thinly
  sliced and loosely packed
3 tablespoons poppy seeds

**Wet ingredients for
batter bread**
1¾ cups potato water
1 tablespoon olive oil

**Wet ingredients for
kneaded bread**
1 cup potato water
1 tablespoon olive oil

**Wet ingredients for
bread machines**
1⅛–1¼ cups potato water as
  required
1 tablespoon olive oil

Steps for batter bread
Mix
1st rise
Stir down, 2nd rise
Bake at 375° for 50 minutes
Test for doneness and cool

Steps for kneaded bread
Mix, knead, oil bowl
1st rise
Punch down, 2nd rise
Shape into loaf, 3rd rise
Crust: poppy seeds
Bake at 400° for 25 minutes
Test for doneness and cool

Crust: topping of poppy seeds
Prepare egg wash: Mix 1 beaten egg with
1 tablespoon milk or water. Before baking,
brush with egg wash, sprinkle with topping,
and brush with egg wash again, using a
patting motion.

Potato Bread with Fresh Rosemary and Shallots

Dry ingredients
3 cups bread flour
1 tablespoon yeast
 (2¼ teaspoons for bread
 machines)
1 teaspoon salt
1 tablespoon sugar
4 tablespoons fresh rosemary,
 chopped small
½ cup shallots, diced small,
 sauteed, and drained

**Wet ingredients for
batter bread**
1¾ cups potato water
1 tablespoon olive oil

**Wet ingredients for
kneaded bread**
1 cup potato water
1 tablespoon olive oil

**Wet ingredients for
bread machines**
1 cup + 2 tablespoons potato
 water
1 tablespoon olive oil

Steps for batter breads
Mix
1st rise
Stir down, 2nd rise
Bake at 375° for 50 minutes
Test for doneness and cool.

Steps for kneaded bread
Mix, knead, oil bowl
1st rise
Punch down, 2nd rise
Shape into loaf, 3rd rise
Crust: chewy
Bake at 400° for 25–30
 minutes
Test for doneness and cool

Crust: chewy
Steam the loaf: Place a pan on the floor of
the oven. Preheat oven to full heat. Toss 6
to 8 ice cubes into the pan, place the loaf in
right away, and close the door quickly.

Roasted Garlic and Chive Potato Bread

Special ingredient (mix in with wet ingredients)
10 cloves of garlic (with skins) roasted in a 450° oven for 10–15 minutes, then minced

Dry ingredients
3 cups bread flour
1 tablespoon yeast
  (2¼ teaspoons for bread machines)
1 teaspoon salt
1 tablespoon sugar
1 cup fresh chives, thinly sliced

Wet ingredients for batter bread
1¾ cups potato water
1 tablespoon olive oil

Wet ingredients for kneaded bread
1 cup potato water
1 tablespoon olive oil

Wet ingredients for bread machines
1⅛–1¼ cups potato water as required
1 tablespoon olive oil

Steps for batter bread
Mix
1st rise
Stir down, 2nd rise
Bake at 375° for 50 minutes
Test for doneness and cool

Steps for kneaded bread
Mix, knead, oil bowl
1st rise
Punch down, 2nd rise
Shape into loaf, 3rd rise
Crust: chives
Bake at 400° for 25 minutes
Test for doneness and cool

Crust: topping of chives, chopped
Prepare egg wash: Mix 1 beaten egg with 1 tablespoon milk or water. Before baking, brush with egg wash, sprinkle with topping, and brush with egg wash again, using a patting motion.

Pimento and Cilantro Potato Bread

Dry ingredients
3 cups bread flour
1 tablespoon yeast
(2¼ teaspoons for bread
machines)
1 teaspoon salt
1 tablespoon sugar
1 4-ounce jar pimentos,
drained and chopped small
½ cup fresh cilantro, chopped
small and packed

Wet ingredients for batter bread
1¾ cups potato water
1 tablespoon olive oil

Wet ingredients for kneaded bread
1 cup potato water
1 tablespoon olive oil

Wet ingredients for bread machines
1⅛–1¼ cups potato water as
required
1 tablespoon olive oil

Steps for batter bread
Mix
1st rise
Stir down, 2nd rise
Bake at 375° for 50 minutes
Test for doneness and cool

Steps for kneaded bread
Mix, knead, oil bowl
1st rise
Punch down, 2nd rise
Shape into loaf, 3rd rise
Crust: chewy
Bake at 400° for 25 minutes
Test for doneness and cool

Crust: chewy
Steam the loaf: Place a pan on the floor of
the oven. Preheat oven to full heat. Toss 6
to 8 ice cubes into the pan, place the loaf in
right away, and close the door quickly.

Herb Potato Bread

Dry ingredients
3 cups bread flour
1 tablespoon yeast
(2¼ teaspoons for bread machines)
1 teaspoon salt
1 tablespoon sugar
¼ cup each fresh cilantro, parsley, oregano, basil, rosemary, and thyme, chopped small and packed

Wet ingredients for batter bread
1¾ cups potato water
1 tablespoon olive oil

Wet ingredients for kneaded bread
1 cup potato water
1 tablespoon olive oil

Wet ingredients for bread machines
1⅛–1¼ cups potato water as required
1 tablespoon olive oil

Steps for batter bread
Mix
1st rise
Stir down, 2nd rise
Bake at 375° for 50 minutes
Test for doneness and cool

Steps for kneaded bread
Mix, knead, oil bowl
1st rise
Punch down, 2nd rise
Shape into loaf, 3rd rise
Crust: soft
Bake at 400° for 25 minutes
Test for doneness and cool

Crust: soft
Brush loaf with milk *before* baking.
 Or
Brush loaf with melted butter *after* baking.

Sweet Potato Bread

Dry ingredients
3 cups bread flour
1 tablespoon yeast
  (2¼ teaspoons for bread
  machines)
1 teaspoon salt
1 tablespoon sugar
1½ tablespoons pumpkin spice

Wet ingredients for batter bread
1 cup sweet potato, cooked
  and mashed with 1½ cups
  of milk
1 tablespoon olive oil

Wet ingredients for kneaded bread
1 cup sweet potato, cooked
  and mashed with ¾ cup
  of milk
1 tablespoon olive oil

Wet ingredients for bread machines
1 cup sweet potato, cooked
  and mashed with 1 cup
  of milk
1 tablespoon olive oil

Steps for batter bread
Mix
1st rise
Stir down, 2nd rise
Bake at 375° for 50 minutes
Test for doneness and cool

Steps for kneaded bread
Mix, knead, oil bowl
1st rise
Punch down, 2nd rise
Shape into loaf, 3rd rise
Crust: toasted pumpkin seeds
Bake at 400° for 25 minutes
Test for doneness and cool

Crust: topping of toasted pumpkin seeds, coarsely chopped
Prepare egg wash: Mix 1 beaten egg with
1 tablespoon milk or water. Before baking, brush
with egg wash, sprinkle with topping, and brush with
egg wash again, using a patting motion.

VI
Whole Grain Breads

You will notice that I use 2 cups of white flour to 1 cup of whole grain flour. This is my personal preference because I like a lighter bread. If you enjoy a denser, chewier bread, try the 100% whole wheat bread recipe on page 102. If you want all of your whole grain breads more dense and chewy, simply omit the white flour and use whole grain flour instead, or increase the proportion of whole grain to white flour. With a higher proportion of whole grain, the dough will take longer to rise.

You will notice that I use honey in all the whole grain recipes. The honey helps make a softer crumb and aids in preserving the bread. If you want a bread that is less sweet, use less honey—1 to 2 tablespoons is enough. If you do reduce the honey, 1 or 2 table-spoons of extra liquid may be needed, depending on the flour.

When selecting a whole wheat flour for breadmaking, do not buy whole wheat pastry flour, which is made from soft winter wheat and has too little gluten for breadmaking. Whole wheat bread flour is made from hard spring wheat. Bread flour made from Deaf Smith County (Texas) wheat is especially good and is carried by most health food stores.

Whole Wheat Bread

Dry ingredients
2 cups bread flour
1 cup whole wheat bread flour
1 tablespoon yeast
  (2¼ teaspoons for bread
  machines)
1 teaspoon salt

**Wet ingredients for
batter bread**
1⅔ cups water
1 tablespoon olive oil
¼ cup honey

**Wet ingredients for
kneaded bread**
⅔ cup water
1 tablespoon olive oil
¼ cup honey

**Wet ingredients for
bread machines**
1 cup water
1 tablespoon olive oil
¼ cup honey

Steps for batter bread
Mix
1st rise
Stir down, 2nd rise
Bake at 375⁰ for 50 minutes
Test for doneness and cool

Steps for kneaded bread
Mix, knead, oil bowl
1st rise
Punch down, 2nd rise
Shape into loaf, 3rd rise
Crust: soft
Bake at 400⁰ for 25 minutes
Test for doneness and cool

Crust: soft
Brush loaf with milk *before* baking.
  Or
Brush loaf with melted butter *after* baking.

Edith's 100 Percent Whole Wheat Bread

This fine lady is 82 years old and still makes her favorite bread. There is a trick to it (as she says). See below in the 2nd rise.

Dry ingredients
3 cups whole wheat bread flour
1 tablespoon yeast
  (2¼ teaspoons for bread
  machines)
1 teaspoon salt

Wet ingredients for batter bread
1¾ cups water
1 tablespoon olive oil
¼ cup honey

Wet ingredients for kneaded bread
1 cup water
1 tablespoon olive oil
¼ cup honey

Wet ingredients for bread machines
1 cup + 2 tablespoons water
1 tablespoon olive oil
¼ cup honey

Steps for batter bread
Mix
1st rise
Stir down, 2nd rise
Bake at 375° for 50 minutes
Test for doneness and cool

Steps for kneaded bread
Mix, knead, oil bowl
1st rise
Punch down, 2nd rise
Shape into loaf, bake
  immediately
Crust: soft
Bake at 400° for 25 minutes
Test for doneness and cool

Crust: soft
Brush loaf with milk *before* baking.
  Or
Brush loaf with melted butter *after* baking.

Cracked Wheat Bread

Dry ingredients
2 cups bread flour
1 cup cracked wheat flour
1 tablespoon yeast
 (2¼ teaspoons for bread
 machines)
1 teaspoon salt

**Wet ingredients for
batter bread**
1¾ cups water
1 tablespoon olive oil
¼ cup honey

**Wet ingredients for
kneaded bread**
1 cup water
1 tablespoon olive oil
¼ cup honey

**Wet ingredients for
bread machines**
1⅛–1¼ cups water as required
1 tablespoon olive oil
¼ cup honey

Steps for batter bread
Mix
1st rise
Stir down, 2nd rise
Bake at 375° for 50 minutes
Test for doneness and cool.

Steps for kneaded bread
Mix, knead, oil bowl
1st rise
Punch down, 2nd rise
Shape into loaf, 3rd rise
Crust: cracked wheat
Bake at 400° for 25 minutes
Test for doneness and cool

Crust: topping of cracked wheat
Prepare egg wash: Mix 1 beaten egg with
1 tablespoon milk or water. Before baking,
brush with egg wash, sprinkle with topping,
and brush with egg wash again, using a
patting motion.

Granola, Bran, and Whole Wheat Bread

Dry ingredients
2 cups bread flour
1 cup whole wheat bread flour
1 tablespoon yeast
(2¼ teaspoons for bread
machines)
1 teaspoon salt
1 cup granola
½ cup bran (oat or wheat)

**Wet ingredients for
batter bread**
2½ cups water
¼ cup honey
1 tablespoon olive oil
1 egg, beaten

**Wet ingredients for
kneaded bread**
1½ cups water
¼ cup honey
1 tablespoon olive oil
1 egg, beaten

**Wet ingredients for
bread machines**
1¾ cups water
¼ cup honey
1 tablespoon olive oil
1 egg, beaten

Steps for batter bread
Mix
1st rise
Stir down, 2nd rise
Bake at 375° for 50 minutes
Test for doneness and cool

Steps for kneaded bread
Mix, knead, oil bowl
1st rise
Punch down, 2nd rise
Shape into loaf, 3rd rise
Crust: bran
Bake at 400° for 25 minutes
Test for doneness and cool

Crust: topping of bran
Prepare egg wash: Mix 1 beaten egg with 1
tablespoon milk or water. Before baking, brush
with egg wash and sprinkle with topping.

Whole Wheat Oat Bran Bread

Dry ingredients
2 cups bread flour
1 cup whole wheat bread flour
1 tablespoon yeast
  (2 ¼ teaspoons for bread
  machines)
1 teaspoon salt
¾ cup oat bran

Wet ingredients for batter bread
1 ¾ cups water
¼ cup honey
1 tablespoon olive oil
2 eggs, beaten
2–3 tablespoons water,
  if needed

Wet ingredients for kneaded bread
1 cup water
¼ cup honey
1 tablespoon olive oil
2 eggs, beaten
2–3 tablespoons water,
  if needed

Wet ingredients for bread machines
1 cup + 2 tablespoons water
¼ cup honey
1 tablespoon olive oil
2 eggs, beaten
2–3 tablespoons water,
  if needed

Steps for batter bread
Mix
1st rise
Stir down, 2nd rise
Bake at 375° for 50 minutes
Test for doneness and cool

Steps for kneaded bread
Mix, knead, oil bowl
1st rise
Punch down, 2nd rise
Shape into loaf, 3rd rise
Crust: oat bran
Bake at 400° for 25 minutes
Test for doneness and cool

Crust: topping of oat bran
Prepare egg wash: Mix 1 beaten egg with 1 tablespoon milk or water. Before baking, brush with egg wash and sprinkle with topping.

Oatmeal Whole Wheat Bread with Seeds

Dry ingredients
2 cups bread flour
1 cup whole wheat bread flour
1 tablespoon yeast
  (2 $\frac{1}{4}$ teaspoons for bread machines)
1 teaspoon salt
2 tablespoons each sesame and poppy seeds
2 tablespoons each pumpkin and sunflower seeds, coarsely chopped
$\frac{1}{2}$ cup quick oats

Wet ingredients for batter bread
2 cups water
3 tablespoons honey
1 tablespoon olive oil
2 eggs, beaten

Wet ingredients for kneaded bread
1 cup + 3 tablespoons water
3 tablespoons honey
1 tablespoon olive oil
2 eggs, beaten

Wet ingredients for bread machines
1 $\frac{1}{4}$ cups water
3 tablespoons honey
1 tablespoon olive oil
2 eggs, beaten

Steps for batter bread
Mix
1st rise
Stir down, 2nd rise
Bake at 375° for 50 minutes
Test for doneness and cool

Steps for kneaded bread
Mix, knead, oil bowl
1st rise
Punch down, 2nd rise
Shape into loaf, 3rd rise
Crust: a sprinkle of seeds and oats
Bake at 400° for 25 minutes
Test for doneness and cool

Crust: topping of rolled oats, sesame seeds, and poppy seeds
Prepare egg wash: Mix 1 beaten egg with 1 tablespoon milk or water. Before baking, brush with egg wash, sprinkle with topping, and brush with egg wash again, using a patting motion.

Cornmeal and Whole Wheat Herb Bread

Dry ingredients
2 cups bread flour
½ cup each cornmeal and
    whole wheat bread flour
1 tablespoon yeast
    (2¼ teaspoons for bread
    machines)
1 teaspoon salt
¼ cup each fresh sage,
    rosemary, and thyme,
    chopped small and packed

**Wet ingredients for
batter bread**
1¾ cups water
¼ cup honey
1 tablespoon olive oil
1 egg, beaten

**Wet ingredients for
kneaded bread**
1 cup water
¼ cup honey
1 tablespoon
1 egg, beaten

**Wet ingredients for
bread machines**
1⅛–1¼ cups water as required
¼ cup honey
1 tablespoon olive oil
1 egg, beaten

Steps for batter breads
Mix
1st rise
Stir down, 2nd rise
Bake at 375° for 50 minutes
Test for doneness and cool

Steps for kneaded bread
Mix, knead, oil bowl
1st rise
Punch down, 2nd rise
Shape into loaf, 3rd rise
Crust: cornmeal
Bake at 400° for 25 minutes
Test for doneness and cool

Crust: topping of cornmeal
Prepare egg wash: Mix 1 beaten egg with 1
tablespoon milk or water. Before baking, brush
with egg wash and sprinkle with topping.

Anadama Bread

As the story goes, the name represents how Anna's husband felt about her constant use of cornmeal. When asked if she could do something different with the cornmeal besides making gruel, she made a bread. Her husband's response was: "Anna, damn her!"

Dry ingredients
1½ cups bread flour
¾ cup whole wheat bread flour
½ cup cornmeal
1 tablespoon yeast
  (2¼ teaspoons for bread
  machines)
1 teaspoon salt

**Wet ingredients for
batter bread**
1¾ cups water
4 tablespoons olive oil
⅓ cup dark molasses

**Wet ingredients for
kneaded bread**
1 cup water
4 tablespoons olive oil
⅓ cup dark molasses

**Wet ingredients for
bread machines**
1⅛–1¼ cups water as required
4 tablespoons olive oil
⅓ cup dark molasses

Steps for batter bread
Mix
1st rise
Stir down, 2nd rise
Bake at 375° for 50 minutes
Test for doneness and cool

Steps for kneaded bread
Mix, knead, oil bowl
1st rise
Punch down, 2nd rise
Shape into loaf, 3rd rise
Crust: soft
Bake at 400° for 25 minutes
Test for doneness and cool

Crust: soft
Brush loaf with milk *before* baking.
  Or
Brush loaf with melted butter *after* baking.

Buckwheat Bread

Dry ingredients
2 cups bread flour
1 cup buckwheat flour
1 tablespoon yeast
   (2 $\frac{1}{4}$ teaspoons for bread
   machines)
1 teaspoon salt

Wet ingredients for batter bread
1 $\frac{3}{4}$ cups water
$\frac{1}{2}$ cup honey
1 tablespoon melted butter

Wet ingredients for kneaded bread
1 cup water
$\frac{1}{2}$ cup honey
1 tablespoon melted butter

Wet ingredients for bread machines
1 $\frac{1}{8}$–1 $\frac{1}{4}$ cups water as required
$\frac{1}{2}$ cup honey
1 tablespoon melted butter

Steps for batter bread
Mix
1st rise
Stir down, 2nd rise
Bake at 375^0 for 50 minutes
Test for doneness and cool

Steps for kneaded bread
Mix, knead, oil bowl
1st rise
Punch down, 2nd rise
Shape into loaf, 3rd rise
Crust: soft
Bake at 400^0 for 25 minutes
Test for doneness and cool

Crust: soft
Brush loaf with milk *before* baking.
   Or
Brush loaf with melted butter *after* baking.

Molasses and Walnut Buckwheat Bread

Dry ingredients
2 cups bread flour
1 cup buckwheat flour
1 tablespoon yeast
  (2¼ teaspoons for bread
  machines)
1 teaspoon salt
1 cup black walnuts,
  chopped small

Wet ingredients for batter bread
1½ cups water
½ cup dark molasses

Wet ingredients for kneaded bread
¾ cup water
½ cup dark molasses

Wet ingredients for bread machines
1 cup water
½ cup dark molasses

Steps for batter bread
Mix
1st rise
Stir down, 2nd rise
Bake at 375° for 50 minutes
Test for doneness and cool

Steps for kneaded bread
Mix, knead, oil bowl
1st rise
Punch down, 2nd rise
Shape into loaf, 3rd rise
Crust: soft
Bake at 400° for 25 minutes
Test for doneness and cool

Crust: soft
Brush loaf with milk *before* baking.
  Or
Brush loaf with melted butter *after* baking.

Whole Wheat Potato Bread

Dry ingredients
2 cups bread flour
1 cup whole wheat bread flour
1 tablespoon yeast
  (2¼ teaspoons for bread
  machines)
1 teaspoon salt
½ cup dried potato flakes

**Wet ingredients for
batter bread**
1¾ cups water
3 tablespoons honey
1 tablespoon olive oil

**Wet ingredients for
kneaded bread**
1 cup water
3 tablespoons honey
1 tablespoon olive oil

**Wet ingredients for
bread machines**
1⅛–1¼ cups water as required
3 tablespoons honey
1 tablespoon olive oil

Steps for batter bread
Mix
1st rise
Stir down, 2nd rise
Bake at 375° for 50 minutes
Test for doneness and cool

Steps for kneaded bread
Mix, knead, oil bowl
1st rise
Punch down, 2nd rise
Shape into loaf, 3rd rise
Crust: soft
Bake at 400° for 25 minutes
Test for doneness and cool

Variation: Wet ingredients:
substitute potato water for
water.

Crust: soft
Brush loaf with milk *before* baking.
  Or
Brush loaf with melted butter *after* baking.

Multi-Grain Bread

Dry ingredients
2¼ cups bread flour
¼ cup each rice, rye, and
 millet flour
1 tablespoon yeast
 (2¼ teaspoons for bread
 machines)
1 teaspoon salt

**Wet ingredients for
batter bread**
1¾ cups water
¼ cup honey
1 tablespoon olive oil

**Wet ingredients for
kneaded bread**
1 cup water
¼ cup honey
1 tablespoon olive oil

**Wet ingredients for
bread machines**
1⅛–1¼ cups water as required
¼ cup honey
1 tablespoon olive oil

Steps for batter bread
Mix
1st rise
Stir down, 2nd rise
Bake at 375⁰ for 50 minutes
Test for doneness and cool

Steps for kneaded bread
Mix, knead, oil bowl
1st rise
Punch down, 2nd rise
Shape into loaf, 3rd rise
Crust: cornmeal
Bake at 400⁰ for 25 minutes
Test for doneness and cool

Crust: topping of cornmeal
Prepare egg wash: Mix 1 beaten egg with 1
tablespoon milk or water. Before baking, brush
with egg wash and sprinkle with topping.

Irish Soda Whole Wheat Bread with Caraway

Dry ingredients
2 cups bread flour
1 cup whole wheat bread flour
1 tablespoon yeast
  (2¼ teaspoons for bread
  machines)
1 teaspoon salt
½ teaspoon baking soda
1 tablespoon caraway seeds

**Wet ingredients for
batter bread**
1¾ cups buttermilk
¼ cup honey
1 tablespoon melted butter

**Wet ingredients for
kneaded bread**
1 cup buttermilk
¼ cup honey
1 tablespoon melted butter

**Wet ingredients for
bread machines**
1¼ cups buttermilk
¼ cup honey
1 tablespoon melted butter

Steps for batter bread
Mix
1st rise
Stir down, 2nd rise
Bake at 375° for 50 minutes
Test for doneness and cool

Steps for kneaded bread
Mix, knead, oil bowl
1st rise
Punch down, 2nd rise
Shape into loaf, 3rd rise
Crust: caraway seeds
Bake at 400° degrees, 25
  minutes
Test for doneness and cool

Crust: topping of caraway seeds
Prepare egg wash: Mix 1 beaten egg with
1 tablespoon milk or water. Before baking,
brush with egg wash, sprinkle with topping,
and brush with egg wash again, using a
patting motion.

Sunflower Seed Whole Wheat Bread

Dry ingredients
2 cups bread flour
1 cup whole wheat bread flour
1 tablespoon yeast
  (2 $\frac{1}{4}$ teaspoons for bread
  machines)
1 teaspoon salt
$\frac{1}{2}$ cup sunflower seeds,
  coarsely chopped

**Wet ingredients for
batter bread**
1 $\frac{2}{3}$ cups water
1 tablespoon olive oil
3 tablespoons honey

**Wet ingredients for
kneaded bread**
$\frac{2}{3}$ cup water
1 tablespoon olive oil
3 tablespoons honey

**Wet ingredients for
bread machines**
1 cup water
1 tablespoon olive oil
3 tablespoons honey

Steps for batter bread
Mix
1st rise
Stir down, 2nd rise
Bake at 375° for 50 minutes
Test for doneness and cool

Steps for kneaded bread
Mix, knead, oil bowl
1st rise
Punch down, 2nd rise
Shape into loaf, 3rd rise
Crust: sunflower seeds
Bake at 400° for 25 minutes
Test for doneness and cool

Crust: topping of sunflower seeds
Prepare egg wash: Mix 1 beaten egg with
1 tablespoon milk or water. Before baking, brush
with egg wash, sprinkle with topping, and brush with
egg wash again, using a patting motion.

Almond, Cardamom, Whole Wheat Bread

Dry ingredients

2 cups bread flour

1 cup whole wheat bread flour

1 tablespoon yeast
(2¼ teaspoons for bread machines)

1 teaspoon salt

1½ tablespoons cardamom seeds, finely crushed

1 cup almond slivers

Wet ingredients for batter bread

1⅔ cups water

1 tablespoon olive oil

¼ cup honey

Wet ingredients for kneaded bread

⅔ cup water

1 tablespoon olive oil

¼ cup honey

Wet ingredients for bread machines

1 cup water

1 tablespoon olive oil

¼ cup honey

Steps for batter bread

Mix

1st rise

Stir down, 2nd rise

Bake at 375° for 50 minutes

Test for doneness and cool

Steps for kneaded bread

Mix, knead, oil bowl

1st rise

Punch down, 2nd rise

Shape into loaf, 3rd rise

Crust: almonds

Bake at 400° for 25 minutes

Test for doneness and cool

Crust: topping of almonds, coarsely chopped
Prepare egg wash: Mix 1 beaten egg with
1 tablespoon milk or water. Before baking, brush
with egg wash, sprinkle with topping, and brush with
egg wash again, using a patting motion.

Wheat and Sprouts Bread

Dry ingredients
2 cups bread flour
1 cup whole wheat bread flour
1 tablespoon yeast
(2¼ teaspoons for bread
machines)
1 teaspoon salt
3 cups sprouts, chopped and
loosely packed

**Wet ingredients for
batter bread**
1⅔ cups water
3 tablespoons honey
1 tablespoon olive oil

**Wet ingredients for
kneaded bread**
⅔ cup water
3 tablespoons honey
1 tablespoon olive oil

**Wet ingredients for
bread machines**
1 cup water
3 tablespoons honey
1 tablespoon olive oil

Steps for batter bread
Mix
1st rise
Stir down, 2nd rise
Bake at 375° for 50 minutes
Test for doneness and cool

Steps for kneaded bread
Mix, knead, oil bowl
1st rise
Punch down, 2nd rise
Shape into loaf, 3rd rise
Crust: poppy seeds
Bake at 400° for 25 minutes
Test for doneness and cool

Crust: topping of poppy seeds
Prepare egg wash: Mix 1 beaten egg with
1 tablespoon milk or water. Before baking,
brush with egg wash, sprinkle with topping,
and brush with egg wash again, using a
patting motion.

Onion and Poppy Seed Whole Wheat Bread

Dry ingredients
2 cups bread flour
1 cup whole wheat bread flour
1 tablespoon yeast
(2¼ teaspoons for bread machines)
1 teaspoon salt
1 cup green onion, thinly sliced and packed
3 tablespoons poppy seeds

Wet ingredients for batter bread
1¾ cups water
3 tablespoons honey
1 tablespoon olive oil

Wet ingredients for kneaded bread
1 cup water
3 tablespoons honey
1 tablespoon olive oil

Wet ingredients for bread machines
1⅛–1¼ cups water as required
3 tablespoons honey
1 tablespoon olive oil

Steps for batter bread
Mix
1st rise
Stir down, 2nd rise
Bake at 375° for 50 minutes
Test for doneness and cool

Steps for kneaded bread
Mix, knead, oil bowl
1st rise
Punch down, 2nd rise
Shape into loaf, 3rd rise
Crust: poppy seeds
Bake at 400° for 25 minutes
Test for doneness and cool

Crust: topping of poppy seeds
Prepare egg wash: Mix 1 beaten egg with 1 tablespoon milk or water. Before baking, brush with egg wash, sprinkle with topping, and brush with egg wash again, using a patting motion.

Onion and Bell Pepper Whole Wheat Bread

Dry ingredients
2 cups bread flour
1 cup whole wheat bread flour
1 tablespoon yeast
(2¼ teaspoons for bread machines)
1 teaspoon salt
½ cup red onion, diced small
½ cup red bell pepper, diced small

Wet ingredients for batter bread
1¾ cups water
3 tablespoons honey
1 tablespoon olive oil

Wet ingredients for kneaded bread
¾ cup water
3 tablespoons honey
1 tablespoon olive oil

Wet ingredients for bread machines
1 cup water
1 tablespoon honey
1 tablespoon olive oil

Steps for batter bread
Mix
1st rise
Stir down, 2nd rise
Bake at 375° for 50 minutes
Test for doneness and cool

Steps for kneaded bread
Mix, knead, oil bowl
1st rise
Punch down, 2nd rise
Shape into loaf, 3rd rise
Crust: soft
Bake at 400° for 25 minutes
Test for doneness and cool

Crust: soft
Brush loaf with milk *before* baking.
 Or
Brush loaf with melted butter *after* baking.

Carrot, Onion, and Sage Whole Wheat Bread

Dry ingredients
2 cups bread flour
1 cup whole wheat bread flour
1 tablespoon yeast
(2¼ teaspoons for bread machines)
1 teaspoon salt
⅔ cup carrots, grated
½ cup green onion, thinly sliced and packed
¼ cup fresh sage, coarsely chopped and packed

Wet ingredients for batter bread
1¾ cups water
3 tablespoons honey
1 tablespoon olive oil

Wet ingredients for kneaded bread
1 cup water
3 tablespoons honey
1 tablespoon olive oil

Wet ingredients for bread machines
1⅛–1¼ cups water as required
3 tablespoons honey
1 tablespoon olive oil

Steps for batter bread
Mix
1st rise
Stir down, 2nd rise
Bake at 375° for 50 minutes
Test for doneness and cool

Steps for kneaded bread
Mix, knead, oil bowl
1st rise
Punch down, 2nd rise
Shape into loaf, 3rd rise
Crust: chewy
Bake at 400° for 25 minutes
Test for doneness and cool

Crust: chewy
Steam the loaf: Place a pan on the floor of the oven. Preheat oven to full heat. Toss 6 to 8 ice cubes into the pan, place the loaf in right away, and close the door quickly.

French-Fried Onion Whole Wheat Bread

Dry ingredients
2 cups bread flour
1 cup whole wheat bread flour
1 tablespoon yeast
  (2 1/4 teaspoons for bread
  machines)
1 teaspoon salt
1 5-ounce can french-fried
  onions, crushed small

**Wet ingredients for
batter bread**
1 3/4 cups water
3 tablespoons honey
1 tablespoon olive oil

**Wet ingredients for
kneaded bread**
1 cup water
3 tablespoons honey
1 tablespoon olive oil

**Wet ingredients for
bread machines**
1 1/8–1 1/4 cups water as required
3 tablespoons honey
1 tablespoon olive oil

Steps for batter bread
Mix
1st rise
Stir down, 2nd rise
Bake at 375° for 50 minutes
Test for doneness and cool

Steps for kneaded bread
Mix, knead, oil bowl
1st rise
Punch down, 2nd rise
Shape into loaf, 3rd rise
Crust: sesame seeds
Bake at 400° for 25 minutes
Test for doneness and cool

Crust: topping of sesame seeds
Prepare egg wash: Mix 1 beaten egg with
1 tablespoon milk or water. Before baking,
brush with egg wash, sprinkle with topping,
and brush with egg wash again, using a
patting motion.

Cheesy Southwest Bread

Dry ingredients

2 cups bread flour

1 cup whole wheat bread flour

1 tablespoon yeast
   (2¼ teaspoons for bread
   machines)

1 teaspoon salt

1 cup Monterey Jack cheese,
   shredded

½ cup hot chile pepper (your
   choice), chopped small and
   loosely packed

1 tablespoon chile powder

1 teaspoon cumin powder

**Wet ingredients for
batter bread**

1¾ cups water

2 tablespoons honey

**Wet ingredients for
kneaded bread**

1 cup water

2 tablespoons honey

**Wet ingredients for
bread machines**

1⅛–1¼ cups water as required

2 tablespoons honey

Steps for batter bread

Mix

1st rise

Stir down, 2nd rise

Bake at 375⁰ for 50 minutes

Test for doneness and cool

Steps for kneaded bread

Mix, knead, oil bowl

1st rise

Punch down, 2nd rise

Shape into loaf, 3rd rise

Crust: soft

Bake at 400⁰ for 25 minutes

Test for doneness and cool

Crust: soft

Brush loaf with milk *before* baking.
   Or
Brush loaf with melted butter *after* baking.

Dark Beer, Onion, and Cheese Whole Wheat Bread

Dry ingredients

2 cups bread flour

1 cup whole wheat bread flour

1 tablespoon yeast
(2¼ teaspoons for bread machines)

1 teaspoon salt

1 cup American cheese, shredded

1 cup red onion, diced small, sauteed, and drained

Wet ingredients for batter bread

1¾ cups dark beer

Wet ingredients for kneaded bread

1 cup dark beer

Wet ingredients for bread machines

1⅛–1¼ cups dark beer
as required

Steps for batter bread

Mix

1st rise

Stir down, 2nd rise

Bake at 375° for 50 minutes

Test for doneness and cool

Steps for kneaded bread

Mix, knead, oil bowl

1st rise

Punch down, 2nd rise

Shape into loaf, 3rd rise

Crust: soft

Bake at 400° for 25 minutes

Test for doneness and cool

Crust: soft

Brush loaf with milk *before* baking.

Or

Brush loaf with melted butter *after* baking.

Whole Wheat Olive and Cream Cheese Bread

Dry ingredients
2 cups bread flour
1 cup whole wheat bread flour
1 tablespoon yeast
  (2¼ teaspoons for bread machines)
1 teaspoon salt
1 cup green salad olives with pimento, chopped small

Wet ingredients for batter bread
1¾ cups water
½ cup cream cheese (room temperature)

Wet ingredients for kneaded bread
1 cup water
½ cup cream cheese (room temperature)

Wet ingredients for bread machines
1⅛–1¼ cups water as required
½ cup cream cheese (room temperature)

Steps for batter bread
Mix
1st rise
Stir down, 2nd rise
Bake at 375° for 50 minutes
Test for doneness and cool

Steps for kneaded bread
Mix, knead, oil bowl
1st rise
Punch down, 2nd rise
Shape into loaf, 3rd rise
Crust: green olives, thinly sliced
Bake at 400° for 25 minutes
Test for doneness and cool

Crust: topping of green olives, thinly sliced
Prepare egg wash: Mix 1 beaten egg with 1 tablespoon milk or water. Before baking, brush with egg wash, sprinkle with topping, and brush with egg wash again, using a patting motion.

Beer and Herb Whole Wheat Bread

Dry ingredients
2 cups bread flour
1 cup whole wheat bread flour
1 tablespoon yeast
(2¼ teaspoons for bread
machines)
1 teaspoon salt
¼ cup each fresh cilantro,
basil, oregano, and rosemary,
chopped small and packed

**Wet ingredients for
batter bread**
1¾ cups beer
1 tablespoon olive oil
1 tablespoon honey

**Wet ingredients for
kneaded bread**
1 cup beer
1 tablespoon olive oil
3 tablespoons honey

**Wet ingredients for
bread machines**
1⅛–1¼ cups beer as required
1 tablespoon olive oil
3 tablespoons honey

Steps for batter bread
Mix
1st rise
Stir down, 2nd rise
Bake at 375° for 50 minutes
Test for doneness and cool

Steps for kneaded bread
Mix, knead, oil bowl
1st rise
Punch down, 2nd rise
Shape into loaf, 3rd rise
Crust: soft
Bake at 400° for 25 minutes
Test for doneness and cool

Crust: soft
Brush loaf with milk *before* baking.
 Or
Brush loaf with melted butter *after* baking.

Whole Wheat Raisin Bread

Dry ingredients
2 cups bread flour
1 cup whole wheat bread flour
1 tablespoon yeast
   (2¼ teaspoons for bread
   machines)
1 teaspoon salt
1 cup raisins
1 teaspoon cinnamon
   (optional)

Wet ingredients for batter bread
1½ cups water
½ cup honey

Wet ingredients for kneaded bread
¾ cup water
½ cup honey

Wet ingredients for bread machines
1 cup water
½ cup honey

Steps for batter bread
Mix
1st rise
Stir down, 2nd rise
Bake at 375° for 50 minutes
Test for doneness and cool

Steps for kneaded bread
Mix, knead, oil bowl
1st rise
Punch down, 2nd rise
Shape into loaf, 3rd rise
Crust: soft
Bake at 400° for 25 minutes
Test for doneness and cool

Crust: soft
Brush loaf with milk *before* baking.
   Or
Brush loaf with melted butter *after* baking.

Honey Graham Bread

Dry ingredients
2 cups bread flour
1 cup whole graham flour
(found in health food stores)
1 tablespoon yeast
(2¼ teaspoons for bread machines)
1 teaspoon salt

Wet ingredients for batter bread
1⅛ cups water
½ cup honey

Wet ingredients for kneaded bread
⅔ cup water
½ cup honey

Wet ingredients for bread machines
1 cup water
½ cup honey

Steps for batter bread
Mix
1st rise
Stir down, 2nd rise
Bake at 375° for 50 minutes
Test for doneness and cool

Steps for kneaded bread
Mix, knead, oil bowl
1st rise
Punch down, 2nd rise
Shape into loaf, 3rd rise
Crust: soft
Bake at 400° for 25 minutes
Test for doneness and cool

Crust: soft
Brush loaf with milk *before* baking.
Or
Brush loaf with melted butter *after* baking.

Honey Nut Whole Wheat Bread

Dry ingredients

2 cups bread flour

1 cup whole wheat bread flour

1 tablespoon yeast
(2¼ teaspoons for bread
machines)

1 teaspoon salt

1 cup nuts, chopped small

**Wet ingredients for
batter bread**

1¾ cups water

½ cup honey

**Wet ingredients for
kneaded bread**

1 cup water

½ cup honey

**Wet ingredients for
bread machines**

1⅛–1¼ cups water as required

½ cup honey

Steps for batter bread

Mix

1st rise

Stir down, 2nd rise

Bake at 375° for 50 minutes

Test for doneness and cool

Steps for kneaded bread

Mix, knead, oil bowl

1st rise

Punch down, 2nd rise

Shape into loaf, 3rd rise

Crust: soft

Bake at 400° for 25 minutes

Test for doneness and cool

Crust: soft
Brush loaf with milk *before* baking.
  Or
Brush loaf with melted butter *after* baking.

Honey Lemon Poppy Seed Bread

Dry ingredients
2 cups bread flour
1 cup whole wheat bread flour
1 tablespoon yeast
    ($2\frac{1}{4}$ teaspoons for bread
    machines)
1 teaspoon salt
$1\frac{1}{2}$ tablespoons lemon zest
3 tablespoons poppy seeds

Wet ingredients for batter bread
$\frac{3}{4}$ cup water
$\frac{1}{2}$ cup honey
$\frac{1}{2}$ cup lemon juice

Wet ingredients for kneaded bread
3–4 tablespoons water
$\frac{1}{2}$ cup honey
$\frac{1}{2}$ cup lemon juice

Wet ingredients for bread machines
$\frac{1}{4}$ cup water
$\frac{1}{2}$ cup honey
$\frac{1}{2}$ cup lemon juice

Steps for batter bread
Mix
1st rise
Stir down, 2nd rise
Bake at 375° for 50 minutes
Test for doneness and cool

Steps for kneaded bread
Mix, knead, oil bowl
1st rise
Punch down, 2nd rise
Shape into loaf, 3rd rise
Crust: poppy seeds
Bake at 400° for 25 minutes
Test for doneness and cool

Crust: topping of poppy seeds
Prepare egg wash: Mix 1 beaten egg with
1 tablespoon milk or water. Before baking,
brush with egg wash, sprinkle with topping,
and brush with egg wash again, using a
patting motion.

Four-Grain, Four-Nut Honey Bread

Dry ingredients
2 cups bread flour
¼ cup each rice flour, whole
  wheat flour, rye flour and
  wheat germ
1 tablespoon yeast
  (2¼ teaspoons for bread
  machines)
1 teaspoon salt
¼ cup each walnuts, cashews,
  pecans, and brazil nuts,
  chopped small

**Wet ingredients for
batter bread**
1½ cups water
½ cup honey

**Wet ingredients for
kneaded bread**
¾ cup water
½ cup honey

**Wet ingredients for
bread machines**
1 cup water
½ cup honey

Steps for batter bread
Mix
1st rise
Stir down, 2nd rise
Bake at 375° for 50 minutes
Test for doneness and cool

Steps for kneaded bread
Mix, knead, oil bowl
1st rise
Punch down, 2nd rise
Shape into loaf, 3rd rise
Crust: soft
Bake at 400° for 25 minutes
Test for doneness and cool

Crust: soft
Brush loaf with milk *before* baking.
  Or
Brush loaf with melted butter *after* baking.

Maple Whole Wheat Bread

Dry ingredients

2 cups bread flour

1 cup whole wheat bread flour

1 tablespoon yeast
(2¼ teaspoons for bread
machines)

1 teaspoon salt

**Wet ingredients for
batter bread**

1½ cups water

½ cup maple syrup

**Wet ingredients for
kneaded bread**

¾ cup water

½ cup maple syrup

**Wet ingredients for
bread machines**

1 cup water

½ cup maple syrup

Steps for batter bread

Mix

1st rise

Stir down, 2nd rise

Bake at 375⁰ for 50 minutes

Test for doneness and cool

Steps for kneaded bread

Mix, knead, oil bowl

1st rise

Punch down, 2nd rise

Shape into loaf, 3rd rise

Crust: soft

Bake at 400⁰ for 25 minutes

Test for doneness and cool

Crust: soft
Brush loaf with milk *before* baking.
  Or
Brush loaf with melted butter *after* baking.

VII
Rye Breads

Rye is a grain that does well in countries that have cold winters. As an addition to bread it is considered very nourishing, partly because it is digested more slowly than other grains and leaves you feeling full a little longer. Many of the rye breads we enjoy came over—like many of our ancestors—on a boat from Europe, where rye bread is traditional.

You will need 2 parts white flour to 1 part rye flour for these breads because rye has very little gluten. The recipes call for light or dark rye, but either type will do. The very dark breads, such as pumpernickel, call for dark rye but get their very dark color from added ingredients such as molasses, cocoa powder, or instant coffee. Pumpernickel flour is not dark by itself but is a slightly coarser grind of light or dark rye.

See also Rye Starter, and Jewish Sour Onion Rye, in Chapter IX (pp. 178 and 181), for an excellent sourdough rye.

New York Rye

For something so simple, this is an excellent bread.

Dry ingredients
2 cups bread flour
1 cup light rye flour
1 tablespoon yeast
  (2¼ teaspoons for bread
  machines)
1 teaspoon salt
1 tablespoon caraway seeds

**Wet ingredients for
batter bread**
1¾ cups water
2 tablespoons honey
1 tablespoon olive oil

**Wet ingredients for
kneaded bread**
1 cup water
2 tablespoons honey
1 tablespoon olive oil

**Crust: topping of
caraway seeds**
Prepare egg wash: Mix 1
beaten egg with1 table-
spoon milk or water.
Before baking, brush with
egg wash, sprinkle with
topping, and brush with
egg wash again, using a
patting motion.

**Wet ingredients for
bread machines**
1⅛–1¼ cups water as required
2 tablespoons honey
1 tablespoon olive oil

Steps for batter bread
Mix
1st rise
Stir down, 2nd rise
Bake at 375° for 50 minutes
Test for doneness and cool

Steps for kneaded bread
Mix, knead, oil bowl
1st rise
Punch down, 2nd rise
Shape into loaf, 3rd rise
Crust: caraway seeds
Bake 400° for 25 minutes
Test for doneness and cool

Variation: You can add 2
tablespoons of Italian
seasoning for something
different.

Pumpernickel Bread

Dry ingredients
2 cups bread flour
1 cup pumpernickel flour (dark rye)
1 tablespoon yeast
(2¼ teaspoons for bread machines)
1 teaspoon salt
1 tablespoon sugar
2 tablespoons caraway seeds
1 tablespoon instant coffee granules

Wet ingredients for batter bread
1¾ cups water
2 tablespoons olive oil
2½ tablespoons molasses

Wet ingredients for kneaded bread
1 cup water
2 tablespoons olive oil
2½ tablespoons molasses

Wet ingredients for bread machines
1⅛–1¼ cups water as required
2 tablespoons olive oil
2½ tablespoons molasses

Steps for batter bread
Mix
1st rise
Stir down, 2nd rise
Bake at 375⁰ for 50 minutes
Test for doneness and cool

Steps for kneaded bread
Mix, knead, oil bowl
1st rise
Punch down, 2nd rise
Shape into loaf, 3rd rise
Crust: caraway seeds
Bake at 400⁰ for 25 minutes
Test for doneness and cool

Crust: topping of caraway seeds
Prepare egg wash: Mix 1 beaten egg with 1 tablespoon milk or water. Before baking, brush with egg wash, sprinkle with topping, and brush with egg wash again, using a patting motion.

Scandinavian Rye

Dry ingredients
2 cups bread flour
1 cup rye flour
1 tablespoon yeast
(2¼ teaspoons for bread machines)
1 teaspoon salt
1 tablespoon each caraway seeds and fennel seeds, crushed
1 tablespoon orange zest

Wet ingredients for batter bread
1¾ cups water
3 tablespoons olive oil
¼ cup molasses

Wet ingredients for kneaded bread
1 cup water
3 tablespoons olive oil
¼ cup molasses

Wet ingredients for bread machines
1⅛–1¼ cups water
3 tablespoons olive oil
¼ cup molasses

Steps for batter bread
Mix
1st rise
Stir down, 2nd rise
Bake at 375^0 for 50 minutes
Test for doneness and cool

Steps for kneaded bread
Mix, knead, oil bowl
1st rise
Punch down, 2nd rise
Shape into loaf, 3rd rise
Crust: soft
Bake at 400^0 for 25 minutes
Test for doneness and cool

Crust: soft
Brush loaf with milk *before* baking.
  Or
Brush loaf with melted butter *after* baking.

Black Russian Rye

Dry ingredients
2 cups bread flour
1 cup dark rye flour
1 tablespoon yeast
(2¼ teaspoons for bread
machines)
1 teaspoon salt
1 teaspoon sugar
2 tablespoons cocoa powder
1 teaspoon instant coffee
1 tablespoon caraway seeds
½ tablespoon fennel seeds
⅔ cup oat bran
1 teaspoon onion flakes

**Wet ingredients for
batter bread**
2 cups water
1½ tablespoons vinegar
2 tablespoons olive oil
1½ tablespoons barley
malt syrup

**Wet ingredients for
kneaded bread**
1¼ cups water
1½ tablespoons vinegar

2 tablespoons olive oil
1½ tablespoons barley
malt syrup

**Wet ingredients for
bread machines**
1 cup + 2 tablespoons water
1¼ tablespoons vinegar
2 tablespoons olive oil
1½ tablespoons barley
malt syrup

Steps for batter bread
Mix
1st rise
Stir down, 2nd rise
Bake at 375° for 50 minutes
Test for doneness and cool

Steps for kneaded bread
Mix, knead, oil bowl
1st rise
Punch down, 2nd rise
Shape into loaf, 3rd rise
Crust: soft
Bake at 400° for 25 minutes
Test for doneness and cool

Crust: soft
Brush loaf with milk *before* baking.
  Or
Brush loaf with melted butter *after* baking.

Milwaukee Rye

This rye-cornmeal bread is a favorite around our house and makes a good sandwich with coleslaw and corned beef.

First prepare **cooked cornmeal**: Mix 1 cup water with ½ cup cornmeal. Cook, stirring constantly, and cool. Add boiling water (amount listed under wet ingredients) and let cool to 120°. Keep extra warm water handy and add as needed.

Dry ingredients

2 cups bread flour
1 cup dark rye flour
1 tablespoon yeast
   (2¼ teaspoons for bread machines)
1 teaspoon salt
½ cup potato flakes (mashed potatoes)
3 tablespoons caraway seeds

Crust: very chewy
Prepare egg wash: Mix 1 beaten egg with 1 tablespoon milk or water. Before baking, brush with egg wash. Then steam: Place a pan on the floor of the oven. Preheat oven to full heat. Toss 6 to 8 ice cubes into the pan, place the loaf in right away, and close the door quickly.

Wet ingredients for batter bread

1¾ cups boiling water (added to cooked cornmeal)
¼ cup honey

Wet ingredients for kneaded bread

1 cup boiling water (added to cooked cornmeal)
¼ cup honey

Wet ingredients for bread machines

1 cup + 2–3 tablespoons boiling water (added to cooked cornmeal)
¼ cup honey

Steps for batter bread
Mix
1st rise
Stir down, 2nd rise
Bake at 375° for 50 minutes
Test for doneness and cool

Steps for kneaded bread
Mix, knead, oil bowl
1st rise
Punch down, 2nd rise
Shape into loaf, 3rd rise
Crust: very chewy
Bake at 375° for 30–35 minutes
Test for doneness and cool

High-Protein Rye

Dry ingredients
2 cups bread flour
¼ cup each soy flour, wheat
   germ, oat bran
½ cup dark rye flour
1 tablespoon yeast
   (2¼ teaspoons for bread
   machines)
1 teaspoon salt

**Wet ingredients for
batter bread**
1¾ cups water
¼ cup honey
1 tablespoon olive oil

**Wet ingredients for
kneaded bread**
1 cup water
¼ cup honey
1 tablespoon olive oil

**Wet ingredients for
bread machines**
1⅛–1¼ cups water as required
¼ cup honey
1 tablespoon olive oil

Steps for batter bread
Mix
1st rise
Stir down, 2nd rise
Bake at 375° for 50 minutes
Test for doneness and cool

Steps for kneaded bread
Mix, knead, oil bowl
1st rise
Punch down, 2nd rise
Shape into loaf, 3rd rise
Crust: soft
Bake at 400° for 25 minutes
Test for doneness and cool

Crust: soft
Brush loaf with milk *before* baking.
   Or
Brush loaf with melted butter *after* baking.

Dark Onion Rye Bread

Dry ingredients

2 cups bread flour

1 cup dark rye flour

1 tablespoon yeast
(2 $\frac{1}{4}$ teaspoons for bread machines)

1 teaspoon salt

1 cup red onion, diced small, cooked until just brown, and drained

Wet ingredients for batter bread

1 $\frac{3}{4}$ cups water

1 tablespoon olive oil

Wet ingredients for kneaded bread

1 cup water

1 tablespoon olive oil

Wet ingredients for bread machines

1 $\frac{1}{8}$–1 $\frac{1}{4}$ cups water as required

1 tablespoon olive oil

Steps for batter bread

Mix

1st rise

Stir down, 2nd rise

Bake at 375° for 50 minutes

Test for doneness and cool

Steps for kneaded bread

Mix, knead, oil bowl

1st rise

Punch down, 2nd rise

Shape into loaf, 3rd rise

Crust: very chewy

Bake at 400° for 25 minutes

Test for doneness and cool

Variation: Shape round (p. 21). Crust: chewy (p. 22). Steam the loaf: Place a pan on the floor of the oven. Preheat oven to full heat. Toss 6 to 8 ice cubes into the pan and place the loaf in right away, closing the door quickly.

Crust: very chewy

Prepare egg wash: Mix 1 beaten egg with 1 tablespoon milk or water. Before baking, brush with egg wash. Then steam: Place a pan on the floor of the oven. Preheat oven to full heat. Toss 6 to 8 ice cubes into the pan, place the loaf in right away, and close the door quickly.

Sour Cream, Onion Rye

Dry ingredients
2 cups bread flour
1 cup dark rye flour
1 tablespoon yeast
(2¼ teaspoons for bread
machines)
1 teaspoon salt
1 tablespoon sugar
1 cup green onion, thinly sliced
(tops only), loosely packed

**Wet ingredients for
batter bread**
1½ cups water
¾ cup sour cream
1 tablespoon olive oil

**Wet ingredients for
kneaded bread**
½ cup water
½ cup sour cream
1 tablespoon olive oil

**Wet ingredients for
bread machines**
½ cup + 2–3 tablespoons
water
½ cup sour cream
1 tablespoon olive oil

Steps for batter bread
Mix
1st rise
Stir down, 2nd rise
Bake at 375° for 50 minutes
Test for doneness and cool

Steps for kneaded bread
Mix, knead, oil bowl
1st rise
Punch down, 2nd rise
Shape into loaf, 3rd rise
Crust: chewy
Bake at 400° for 25 minutes
Test for doneness and cool

Crust: chewy
Steam the loaf: Place a pan on the floor of
the oven. Preheat oven to full heat. Toss 6
to 8 ice cubes into the pan, place the loaf in
right away, and close the door quickly.

Onion Buttermilk Rye

Dry ingredients

1½ cups bread flour
1 cup rye flour
½ cup whole wheat flour
1 tablespoon yeast
   (2¼ teaspoons for bread
   machines)
1 teaspoon salt
½ teaspoon baking soda
1 cup onions, diced small,
   sauteed, and drained

Wet ingredients for
batter bread

¾ cup water
1 cup buttermilk
1 tablespoon olive oil
3 tablespoons honey

Wet ingredients for
kneaded bread

¼ cup water
¾ cup buttermilk
1 tablespoon olive oil
3 tablespoons honey

Wet ingredients for
bread machines

½ cup water
¾ cup buttermilk
1 tablespoon olive oil
3 tablespoons honey

Steps for batter bread

Mix
1st rise
Stir down, 2nd rise
Bake at 375° for 50 minutes
Test for doneness and cool

Steps for kneaded bread

Mix, knead, oil bowl
1st rise
Punch down, 2nd rise
Shape into loaf, 3rd rise
Crust: chewy
Bake at 400° for 25 minutes
Test for doneness and cool

Crust: chewy
Steam the loaf: Place a pan on the floor of
the oven. Preheat oven to full heat. Toss 6
to 8 ice cubes into the pan, place the loaf in
right away, and close the door quickly.

Soy, Sage, and Onion Rye

Dry ingredients
1½ cups bread flour
1 cup rye flour
¼ cup whole wheat bread flour
¼ cup soy flour
1 tablespoon yeast
 (2¼ teaspoons for bread
 machines)
1 teaspoon salt
¼ cup fresh sage, chopped
 small and loosely packed
1 cup red onion, diced small
½ teaspoon onion powder

**Wet ingredients for
batter bread**
1¾ cups water
2 tablespoons honey
1 tablespoon olive oil

**Wet ingredients for
kneaded bread**
1 cup water
2 tablespoons honey
1 tablespoon olive oil

**Wet ingredients for
bread machines**
1⅛–1¼ cups water as required
2 tablespoons honey
1 tablespoon olive oil

Steps for batter bread
Mix
1st rise
Stir down, 2nd rise
Bake at 375⁰ for 50 minutes
Test for doneness and cool

Steps for kneaded bread
Mix, knead, oil bowl
1st rise
Punch down, 2nd rise
Shape into loaf, 3rd rise
Crust: soft
Bake at 400⁰ for 25 minutes
Test for doneness and cool

Crust: soft
Brush loaf with milk *before* baking.
 Or
Brush loaf with melted butter *after* baking.

Onion Rye with Beer and Cheese

Dry ingredients
1½ cups bread flour
1 cup rye flour
1 tablespoon yeast
(2¼ teaspoons for bread
machines)
1 tablespoon sugar
1 cup onion, chopped,
browned, and drained
1½ cups Colby cheese,
shredded

**Wet ingredients for
batter bread**
1¾ cups beer
1 tablespoon olive oil

**Wet ingredients for
kneaded bread**
1 cup beer
1 tablespoon olive oil

**Wet ingredients for
bread machines**
1 cup + 2 tablespoons beer
1 tablespoon olive oil

Steps for batter bread
Mix
1st rise
Stir down, 2nd rise
Bake at 375° for 50 minutes
Test for doneness and cool

Steps for kneaded bread
Mix, knead, oil bowl
1st rise
Punch down, 2nd rise
Shape into loaf, 3rd rise
Crust: onion, chopped small,
browned, and drained
Bake at 400° for 25 minutes
Test for doneness and cool

**Crust: topping of onion, chopped small, browned,
and drained**
Prepare egg wash: Mix 1 beaten egg with
1 tablespoon milk or water. Before baking, brush
with egg wash, sprinkle with topping, and brush with
egg wash again, using a patting motion.

Swiss Cheese and Spicy Mustard Rye

Dry ingredients
1½ cups bread flour
1 cup light light flour
1 tablespoon yeast
    (2¼ teaspoons for bread
    machines)
1 teaspoon salt
1 cup Swiss cheese, shredded

Wet ingredients for batter bread
1½ cups water
2 tablespoons honey
1 tablespoons olive oil
3 heaping tablespoons spicy
    mustard

Wet ingredients for kneaded bread
¾ cup water
2 tablespoons honey
1 tablespoon olive oil
3 heaping tablespoons spicy
    mustard

Wet ingredients for bread machines
1 cup water
2 tablespoons honey
1 tablespoon olive oil
3 heaping tablespoons spicy
    mustard

Steps for batter bread
Mix
1st rise
Stir down, 2nd rise
Bake at 375° for 50 minutes
Test for doneness and cool

Steps for kneaded bread
Mix, knead, oil bowl
1st rise
Punch down, 2nd rise
Shape into loaf, 3rd rise
Crust: very chewy
Bake at 400° for 25 minutes
Test for doneness and cool

Crust: very chewy
Prepare egg wash: Mix 1 beaten egg with 1 tablespoon milk or water. Before baking, brush with egg wash. Then steam: Place a pan on the floor of the oven. Preheat oven to full heat. Toss 6 to 8 ice cubes into the pan, place the loaf in right away, and close the door quickly.

Pepper and Smoked Cheese Rye

Dry ingredients
2 cups bread flour
1 cup light rye flour
1 tablespoon yeast
  (2¼ teaspoons for bread
  machines)
1 teaspoon salt
1 tablespoon sugar
1 cup firm smoked cheese,
  shredded
1½ tablespoons black pepper
  or to taste

**Wet ingredients for
batter bread**
1¾ cups water
1 tablespoon olive oil

**Wet ingredients for
kneaded bread**
1 cup water
1 tablespoon olive oil

**Wet ingredients for
bread machines**
1⅛–1¼ cups water as required
1 tablespoon olive oil

Steps for batter bread
Mix
1st rise
Stir down, 2nd rise
Bake at 375° for 50 minutes
Test for doneness and cool

Steps for kneaded bread
Mix, knead, oil bowl
1st rise
Punch down, 2nd rise
Shape into loaf, 3rd rise
Crust: cracked black pepper
Bake at 400° for 25 minutes
Test for doneness and cool

Crust: topping of cracked black pepper
Prepare egg wash: Mix 1 beaten egg with 1
tablespoon milk or water. Before baking, brush
with egg wash and sprinkle with topping.

Caraway Beer Rye

Dry ingredients
2 cups bread flour
1 cup light rye flour
1 tablespoon yeast
(2¼ teaspoons for bread
machines)
1 teaspoon salt
3 tablespoons caraway seeds

Wet ingredients for batter bread
1¾ cups beer
1 tablespoon olive oil

Wet ingredients for kneaded bread
1 cup beer
1 tablespoon olive oil

Wet ingredients for bread machines
1⅛–1¼ cups beer as required
1 tablespoon olive oil

Crust: topping of caraway seeds
Prepare egg wash: Mix 1 beaten egg with 1 tablespoon milk or water. Before baking, brush with egg wash, sprinkle with topping, and brush with egg wash again, using a patting motion.

Steps for batter bread
Mix
1st rise
Stir down, 2nd rise
Bake at 375° for 50 minutes
Test for doneness and cool

Steps for kneaded bread
Mix, knead, oil bowl
1st rise
Punch down, 2nd rise
Shape into loaf, 3rd rise
Crust: caraway seeds
Bake at 400° for 25 minutes
Test for doneness and cool

Variation: Shape round (p. 21). Crust: chewy (p. 22) with caraway seeds Use egg wash, as in main recipe. Steam the loaf: Place a pan on the floor of the oven. Preheat oven to full heat. Toss 6 to 8 ice cubes into the pan and place the loaf in right away, closing the door quickly.

Pickle Rye

Not only does this make a good sandwich bread, it is also excellent toasted and spread with cream cheese.

Dry ingredients
2 cups bread flour
1 cup light rye flour
1 tablespoon yeast
    (2 ¼ teaspoons for bread
    machines)
1 teaspoon salt
½ cup red onion, diced small
    (optional)

**Wet ingredients for
batter bread**
1 cup water
¾ cup dill pickle juice
2 tablespoons honey
1 tablespoon olive oil
½ cup dill pickle relish, drained

**Wet ingredients for
kneaded bread**
½ cup water
½ cup dill pickle juice
2 tablespoons honey
1 tablespoon olive oil
½ cup dill pickle relish, drained

Variation: Replace the pickle juice and relish with sauerkraut and sauerkraut juice. This is a wonderful moist bread.

**Wet ingredients for
bread machines**
¾ cup water
½ cup dill pickle juice
2 tablespoons honey
1 tablespoon olive oil
½ cup dill pickle relish, drained

Steps for batter bread
Mix
1st rise
Stir down, 2nd rise
Bake at 375⁰ for 50 minutes
Test for doneness and cool

Steps for kneaded bread
Mix, knead, oil bowl
1st rise
Punch down, 2nd rise
Shape into loaf, 3rd rise
Crust: dill weed
Bake at 400⁰ for 25 minutes
Test for doneness and cool

**Crust: topping of
dill weed**
Prepare egg wash: Mix 1 beaten egg with 1 tablespoon milk or water. Before baking, brush with egg wash and sprinkle with topping.

Garlic Lover's Rye with Dill

Dry ingredients
2 cups bread flour
1 cup rye flour
1 tablespoon yeast
(2¼ teaspoons for bread
machines)
1 teaspoon salt
1 tablespoon sugar
½ teaspoon garlic powder
3 tablespoons dill weed, dried

Wet ingredients for
batter bread
1¾ cups water
⅛ cup garlic, minced
1½ tablespoons melted butter

Wet ingredients for
kneaded bread
1 cup water
⅛ cup garlic, minced
1½ tablespoons melted butter

Wet ingredients for
bread machines
1⅛–1¼ cups water as required
⅛ cup garlic, minced
1½ tablespoons melted butter

Steps for batter bread
Mix
1st rise
Stir down, 2nd rise
Bake at 375° for 50 minutes
Test for doneness and cool

Steps for kneaded bread
Mix, knead, oil bowl
1st rise
Punch down, 2nd rise
Shape into loaf, 3rd rise
Crust: garlic, minced
Bake at 400° for 25 minutes
Test for doneness and cool

Crust: topping of garlic, minced
Prepare egg wash: Mix 1 beaten egg with 1 tablespoon milk or water. Before baking, brush with egg
wash, sprinkle with topping, and brush with egg
wash again, using a patting motion.

Cumin Rye

Dry ingredients
2 cups bread flour
1 cup dark rye flour
1 tablespoon yeast
  ($2\frac{1}{4}$ teaspoons for bread
  machines)
1 teaspoon salt
1 tablespoon sugar
1 tablespoon cumin seeds

Wet ingredients for batter bread
$1\frac{3}{4}$ cups water
1 tablespoon olive oil

Wet ingredients for kneaded bread
1 cup water
1 tablespoon olive oil

Wet ingredients for bread machines
$1\frac{1}{8}$–$1\frac{1}{4}$ cups water as required
1 tablespoon olive oil

Steps for batter bread
Mix
1st rise
Stir down, 2nd rise
Bake at 375^0 for 50 minutes
Test for doneness and cool

Steps for kneaded bread
Mix, knead, oil bowl
1st rise
Punch down, 2nd rise
Shape into loaf, 3rd rise
Crust: cumin seeds
Bake at 400^0 for 25 minutes
Test for doneness and cool

Variation: Shape round (p. 21). Crust: chewy (p. 22) with cumin seeds. Use egg wash, as in main recipe. Steam the loaf: Place a pan on the floor of the oven. Preheat oven to full heat. Toss 6 to 8 ice cubes into the pan and place the loaf in right away, closing the door quickly.

Crust: topping of sesame seeds
Prepare egg wash: Mix 1 beaten egg with 1 tablespoon milk or water. Before baking, brush with egg wash, sprinkle with topping, and brush with egg wash again, using a patting motion.

Ginger Rye

Dry ingredients
2 cups bread flour
1 cup dark rye flour
1 tablespoon yeast
  (2 ¼ teaspoons for bread
  machines)
1 teaspoon salt
1 tablespoon sugar

**Wet ingredients for
batter bread**
1 ¾ cups water
¼ cup fresh ginger, grated
2 tablespoons melted butter

**Wet ingredients for
kneaded bread**
1 cup water
¼ cup fresh ginger, grated
2 tablespoons melted butter

**Wet ingredients for
bread machines**
1 ⅛–1 ¼ cups water as required
¼ cup fresh ginger, grated
2 tablespoons melted butter

Steps for batter bread
Mix
1st rise
Stir down, 2nd rise
Bake at 375° for 50 minutes
Test for doneness and cool

Steps for kneaded bread
Mix, knead, oil bowl
1st rise
Punch down, 2nd rise
Shape into loaf, 3rd rise
Crust: soft
Bake at 400° for 25 minutes
Test for doneness and cool

Crust: soft
Brush loaf with milk *before* baking.
  Or
Brush loaf with melted butter *after* baking.

Veggie Rye

Dry ingredients

2 cups bread flour

1 cup dark rye flour

1 tablespoon yeast
 (2 ¼ teaspoons for bread
 machines)

1 teaspoon salt

1 tablespoon sugar

1 1-ounce package dried
 veggie soup mix

**Wet ingredients for
batter bread**

1 ¾ cups water

1 tablespoon olive oil

**Wet ingredients for
kneaded bread**

1 cup water

1 tablespoon olive oil

**Wet ingredients for
bread machines**

1 ⅛–1 ¼ cups water as required

1 tablespoon olive oil

Steps for batter bread

Mix

1st rise

Stir down, 2nd rise

Bake at 375° for 50 minutes

Test for doneness and cool

Steps for kneaded bread

Mix, knead, oil bowl

1st rise

Punch down, 2nd rise

Shape into loaf, 3rd rise

Crust: chewy

Bake at 400° for 25 minutes

Test for doneness and cool

Crust: chewy
Steam the loaf: Place a pan on the floor of
the oven. Preheat oven to full heat. Toss 6
to 8 ice cubes into the pan, place the loaf in
right away, and close the door quickly.

VIII
Traditional and Ethnic Loaves

Once you have mastered the basics of making bread in a standard loaf pan, you may want to try your hand at baking breads in some of the traditional shapes—Italian or French loaf, a braided loaf, a round or oval loaf, or baguettes and breadsticks. (Traditional yeasted flatbread recipes are given in Chapter XI.) Some recipes in this chapter—such as Swiss Zoph Bread and Challah—are for ethnic breads that are traditionally baked for holidays, but shaped breads are good for any occasion, or just for the fun of developing your personal breadmaking artistry. Once you get the hang of it, you needn't limit yourself to the shapes, crusts, and ingredients in the following recipes. In fact, most recipes for kneaded bread can be made into any shape you want, from a baguette to a bialy.

You will find detailed instructions for creating various loaf shapes on pages 20–21. If you are using a bread machine, remove the dough after the second rise, punch it down, and shape it for baking.

See also Chapter IX, Artisan and Sourdough Breads (p. 168).

Italian Bread

Dry ingredients
3 cups bread flour
1 tablespoon yeast
  (2 ¼ teaspoons for bread
  machines)
1 teaspoon salt

**Wet ingredients for
kneaded bread**
1 cup water

**Wet ingredients for
bread machines**
1 cup + 2 tablespoons water

Steps for kneaded bread
Mix, knead, oil bowl
Note: For a nice open crumb,
  knead lightly just a few times.

1st rise
Punch down, 2nd rise
Shape into Italian loaf (p. 21)
Slash diagonally 4 times,
  3rd rise
Crust: crisp
Bake at 400° for 25–30
  minutes
Test for doneness and cool

Steps for bread machines
Put in bread machine to mix,
  knead, and rise
Remove from machine after
  2nd rise to finish by hand

Crust: crisp
Using a spray bottle, spray the loaf 4
times with cold water during baking.

French Bread

Dry ingredients
3 cups bread flour
1 tablespoon yeast
(2¼ teaspoons for bread
machines)
1 teaspoon salt

**Wet ingredients for
kneaded bread**
1 cup water

**Wet ingredients for
bread machines**
1 cup + 2 tablespoons water

Steps for kneaded bread
Mix, knead, oil bowl

1st rise
Punch down, 2nd rise
Shape into French loaf (p. 21)
Slash diagonally 4 times,
3rd rise
Crust: very chewy, with
sesame seeds
Bake at 400° for 25–30
minutes
Test for doneness and cool

Steps for bread machines
Put in bread machine to mix,
knead, and rise
Remove from machine after
2nd rise to finish by hand

Crust: very chewy, with sesame seeds
Prepare egg wash: Mix 1 beaten egg with 1
tablespoon milk or water. Before baking, brush
with egg wash, sprinkle with sesame seeds, and
brush with egg wash again, using a patting
motion. Then steam: Place a pan on the floor
of the oven. Preheat oven to full heat. Toss 6
to 8 ice cubes into the pan, place the loaf in
right away, and close the door quickly.

Swiss Zoph Bread

Dry ingredients
3 cups bread flour
1 tablespoon yeast
(2¼ teaspoons for bread
machines)
1 teaspoon salt
½ tablespoon sugar

Wet ingredients for kneaded bread
¾ cup water
1 egg + 1 egg yolk, beaten
3 tablespoons melted butter

Wet ingredients for bread machines
¾ cup + 3 tablespoons water
1 egg + 1 egg yolk, beaten
3 tablespoons melted butter

Steps for kneaded bread
Mix, knead, oil bowl
1st rise
Punch down, 2nd rise
Shape into a long braided
loaf (p. 20), 3rd rise
Crust: a sprinkle of salt over
sesame seeds
Bake at 400° for 30–35
minutes
Test for doneness and cool

Steps for bread machines
Put in bread machine to mix,
knead, and rise
Remove from machine after
2nd rise to finish by hand

Crust: topping of sesame seeds and salt
Prepare egg wash: Mix 1 beaten egg with
1 tablespoon milk or water. Before baking,
brush with egg wash, sprinkle with sesame
seeds, and brush with egg wash again, using
a patting motion, then sprinkle with salt.

Pain de Mie

French Pullman Bread

Dry ingredients

3 cups bread flour

1 tablespoon yeast
(2¼ teaspoons for bread machines)

1 teaspoon salt

1 tablespoon sugar

Wet ingredients for kneaded bread

1 cup milk

2 tablespoons melted butter

Wet ingredients for bread machines

1 cup + 2 tablespoons milk

3 tablespoons melted butter

Steps for kneaded bread

Mix, knead, oil bowl

1st rise

Punch down, 2nd rise

Shape into a pullman
loaf (p. 21), 3rd rise

Bake at 400° for 25–30
minutes

Test for doneness and cool

Steps for bread machines

Put in bread machine to mix,
knead, and rise

Remove from machine after
2nd rise to finish by hand

Crusty Cuban Bread

Dry ingredients
3 cups bread flour
1 tablespoon yeast
(2 ¼ teaspoons for bread
machines)
1 teaspoon salt
½ tablespoon sugar

**Wet ingredients for
kneaded bread**
1 cup water

**Wet ingredients for
bread machines**
1 cup + 2 tablespoons water

Steps for kneaded bread
Mix, knead, oil bowl
1st rise
Punch down, 2nd rise

Shape into a long flattened loaf
(page 21
Slash diagonally 4 times,
3rd rise
Crust: Crisp
Bake at 400° for 25–30
minutes
Test for doneness and cool

Steps for bread machines
Put in bread machine to mix,
knead, and rise
Remove from machine after
2nd rise to finish by hand

Crust: crisp
Spray the loaf with cold water
4 times during baking.

Broa

Portuguese Cornbread

Special ingredients

Boil ¾ cup water. Mix ¼ cup cold water and ¼ cup cornstarch and add to boiling water. Simmer for 1 minute, cool to 120°, and add to wet ingredients.

Dry ingredients

2 cups bread flour
1 cup corn flour (*not* cornmeal)
1 tablespoon yeast
   (2¼ teaspoons for bread machines)
1 teaspoon salt

Wet ingredients for kneaded bread

1 cup water
Cornstarch mixture

Wet ingredients for bread machines

1 cup + 2 tablespoons water
Cornstarch mixture

Steps for kneaded bread

Mix, knead, oil bowl
1st rise
Punch down, 2nd rise
Shape into round loaf (p. 00)
Slash an X on the top, 3rd rise
Crust: flour
Bake at 400° for 25–30 minutes. Bake under a foil tent for the first 15 minutes.
Test for doneness and cool

Steps for bread machines

Put in bread machine to mix, knead, and rise
Remove from machine after 2nd rise to finish by hand

Crust: flour
Prepare egg wash: Mix 1 beaten egg with 1 tablespoon milk or water. Before last rise, brush lightly with egg wash and dust heavily with flour.

Bran and Shredded Wheat Bread

Dry ingredients
1½ cups bread flour
½ cup all-bran cereal
1 cup shredded wheat cereal, crushed
1 tablespoon yeast (2¼ teaspoons for bread machines)
1 teaspoon salt
1 tablespoon brown sugar

Wet ingredients for kneaded bread
1 cup water
1 tablespoon olive oil

Wet ingredients for bread machines
1 cup + 2 tablespoons water
1 tablespoon olive oil

Steps for kneaded bread
Mix, knead, oil bowl
1st rise
Punch down, 2nd rise
Shape into round braid (p. 20), 3rd rise
Crust: very chewy, with sesame seeds
Bake at 400° for 25–30 minutes
Test for doneness and cool

Steps for bread machines
Put in bread machine to mix, knead, and rise
Remove from machine after 2nd rise to finish by hand

Crust: very chewy, with sesame seeds
Prepare egg wash: Mix 1 beaten egg with 1 tablespoon milk or water. Before baking, brush with egg wash, sprinkle with sesame seeds, and brush with egg wash again, using a patting motion. Then steam: Place a pan on the floor of the oven. Preheat oven to full heat. Toss 6 to 8 ice cubes into the pan, place the loaf in right away, and close the door quickly.

Confetti Bread

Dry ingredients
3 cups bread flour
1 tablespoon yeast
   (2¼ teaspoons for bread
   machines)
1 teaspoon salt
1 tablespoon sugar
¼ cup each red, yellow, and
   green bell pepper, diced small
¼ cup fresh cilantro, chopped
   small and loosely packed
1 tablespoon onion flakes,
   soaked in ¼ cup warm water
   and drained
1 tablespoon garlic, minced
1 teaspoon celery seed

Wet ingredients for kneaded bread
1 cup water

Wet ingredients for bread machines
1 cup + 2 tablespoons water

Steps for kneaded bread
Mix, knead, oil bowl
1st rise
Punch down, 2nd rise
Shape into round loaf (p. 21)
Slash an X on the top, 3rd rise
   (45 minutes)
Crust: soft
Bake at 350° for 45–55
   minutes
Test for doneness and cool

Steps for bread machines
Put in bread machine to mix,
   knead, and rise
Remove from machine after
   2nd rise to finish by hand

Crust: soft
Brush loaf with milk *before* baking.
   Or
Brush loaf with melted butter *after* baking.

Italian Herb Bread

Dry ingredients
3 cups bread flour
1 tablespoon yeast
 (2¼ teaspoons for bread
 machines)
1 teaspoon salt
1 tablespoon each toasted
 sesame and poppy seeds
2 tablespoons each fresh
 oregano, basil, and cilantro,
 chopped small and packed
1 tablespoon garlic, minced
½ cup red onions, diced small,
 sauteed, and drained.

Wet ingredients for kneaded bread
1 cup water

Wet ingredients for bread machines
1 cup + 2 tablespoons water

Steps for kneaded bread
Mix, knead, oil bowl
1st rise
Punch down, 2nd rise
Shape into Italian loaf (p. 21)
Slash diagonally 4 times,
 3rd rise
Crust: crisp
Bake at 400° for 25–30
 minutes
Test for doneness and cool

Steps for bread machines
Put in bread machine to mix,
 knead, and rise
Remove from machine after
 2nd rise to finish by hand

Crust: crisp
Using a spray bottle, spray the loaf 4
times with cold water during baking.

Green Olive Bread

Dry ingredients
3 cups bread flour
1 tablespoon yeast
   ($2\frac{1}{4}$ teaspoons for bread
   machines)
1 teaspoon salt
1 tablespoon sugar
1 cup green salad olives with
   pimiento, drained and
   coarsely chopped
   (reserve juice)

Wet ingredients for kneaded bread
$\frac{1}{2}$ cup water
$\frac{1}{2}$ cup olive juice

Wet ingredients for bread machines
$\frac{1}{2}$ cup + 2 tablespoons water
$\frac{1}{2}$ cup olive juice

Steps for kneaded bread
Mix, knead, oil bowl
1st rise
Punch down, 2nd rise
Shape into round loaf (p. 21)
Slash X on top, 3rd rise
Crust: sliced green olives
Bake at 400° for 25–30
   minutes
Test for doneness and cool

Steps for bread machines
Put in bread machine to mix,
   knead, and rise
Remove from machine after
   2nd rise to finish by hand

Crust: topping of sliced green olives
Prepare egg wash: Mix 1 beaten egg with
1 tablespoon milk or water. Before baking, brush
with egg wash, sprinkle with topping, and brush with
egg wash again, using a patting motion.

Shaker Herb Bread

Dry ingredients

3 cups bread flour

1 tablespoon yeast
(2¼ teaspoons for bread
machines)

1 teaspoon salt

1 tablespoon sugar

1 teaspoon celery seeds

1 tablespoon caraway seeds

1 tablespoon fresh sage,
coarsely chopped and packed

1 teaspoon nutmeg, ground
(freshly ground if you can
find it)

**Wet ingredients for
kneaded bread**

¾ cup milk

1 egg, beaten

**Wet ingredients for
bread machines**

1 cup milk

1 egg, beaten

Steps for kneaded bread

Mix, knead, oil bowl

1st rise

Punch down, 2nd rise

Shape into oval loaf (p. 21)

Slash diagonally 3 times,
3rd rise

Crust: lots of sesame seeds

Bake at 400° for 25–30
minutes

Test for doneness and cool

Steps for bread machines

Put in bread machine to mix,
knead, and rise

Remove from machine after
2nd rise to finish by hand

Crust: topping of sesame seeds
Prepare egg wash: Mix 1 beaten egg with
1 tablespoon milk or water. Before baking,
brush with egg wash, sprinkle with topping,
and brush with egg wash again, using a
patting motion.

Pesto Bread

Pesto sauce
2 cups fresh basil, coarsely
  chopped and tightly packed
½ cup fresh Parmesan cheese,
  grated
½ cup toasted pine nuts
¼ cup olive oil
Salt and pepper to taste
Put all ingredients in a blender
  and blend until smooth.
Makes about 1½ cups.

Dry ingredients
3 cups bread flour
1 tablespoon yeast
  (2¼ teaspoons for bread
  machines)
1 teaspoon salt
1 tablespoon sugar

Wet ingredients for
kneaded bread
½–¾ cup water as needed
1½ cups pesto sauce

Wet ingredients for
bread machines
1 cup + tablespoons of water
  as required
1½ cups pesto sauce

Steps for kneaded bread
Mix, knead, oil bowl
1st rise
Punch down, 2nd rise
Shape into braided loaf (p. 20),
  3rd rise
Crust: Parmesan cheese
Bake at 400° for 40–45
  minutes
Test for doneness and cool

Steps for bread machines
Put in bread machine to mix,
  knead, and rise
Remove after 2nd rise to finish
  by hand

Crust: topping of Parmesan cheese
Prepare egg wash: Mix 1 beaten egg with 1
tablespoon milk or water. Before baking, brush
with egg wash and sprinkle with topping.

Semolina Bread

Semolina flour is best known for making pasta, but also makes a delicious bread. It is pale yellow in color.

Dry ingredients
2½ cups bread flour
½ cup semolina flour
½ cup durum flour
1 tablespoon yeast
  (2¼ teaspoons for bread
  machines)
1 teaspoon salt
1 tablespoon sugar

**Wet ingredients for
kneaded bread**
1 cup water

**Wet ingredients for
bread machines**
1 cup + 2 tablespoons water

Steps for kneaded bread
Mix, knead, oil bowl
1st rise
Punch down, 2nd rise
Shape into braided circle
  (p. 20), 3rd rise
Crust: poppy seeds
Bake at 450° for 10 minutes,
  then at 350° for 30 minutes
Test for doneness and cool

Steps for bread machines
Put in bread machine to mix,
  knead, and rise
Remove from machine after
  2nd rise to finish by hand

Crust: topping of poppy seeds
Prepare egg wash: Mix 1 beaten egg with
1 tablespoon milk or water. Before baking,
brush with egg wash, sprinkle with topping,
and brush with egg wash again, using a
patting motion.

Braided Sesame Seed Bread

Dry ingredients
3 cups bread flour
1 tablespoon yeast
(2¼ teaspoons for bread
machines)
1 teaspoon salt
1 tablespoon sugar
¼ cup toasted sesame seeds

**Wet ingredients
kneaded bread**
¾ cup water
2 tablespoons sesame seed oil
1 egg, beaten

**Wet ingredients for
bread machines**
1 cup water
2 tablespoons sesame seed oil
1 egg, beaten

Steps for kneaded bread
Mix, knead, oil bowl
1st rise
Punch down, 2nd rise
Shape into braided loaf (p. 20),
3rd rise
Crust: lots of sesame seeds
Bake at 400° for 25–30
minutes
Test for doneness and cool

Steps for bread machines
Put in bread machine to mix,
knead, and rise
Remove from machine after
2nd rise to finish by hand

Crust: topping of sesame seeds
Prepare egg wash: Mix 1 beaten egg with
1 tablespoon milk or water. Before baking,
brush with egg wash, sprinkle with topping,
and brush with egg wash again, using a
patting motion.

Black Pepper and Onion Bread

Dry ingredients
3 cups bread flour
1 tablespoon yeast
(2¼ teaspoons for bread
machines)
1 teaspoon salt
1 tablespoon black pepper or
to taste
1 cup red onions, diced small,
sauteed, and drained

Wet ingredients for kneaded bread
1 cup water

Wet ingredients for bread machines
1 cup + 2 tablespoons water

Steps for kneaded bread
Mix, knead, oil bowl
1st rise
Punch down, 2nd rise
Shape into long oval (p. 21)
Slash diagonally 4 times,
3rd rise
Crust: a sprinkle of
black pepper
Bake at 400° for 25–30
minutes
Test for doneness and cool

Steps for bread machines
Put in bread machine to mix,
knead, and rise
Remove from machine after
2nd rise to finish by hand

Crust: topping of black pepper
Prepare egg wash: Mix 1 beaten egg with 1
tablespoon milk or water. Before baking, brush
with egg wash and sprinkle with topping.

Caraway and Bacon Braided Bread

Dry ingredients
3 cups bread flour
1 tablespoon yeast
  (2¼ teaspoons for bread
  machines)
1 teaspoon salt
1 cup bacon, diced, fried,
  and drained
2 tablespoons caraway seeds,
  or to taste

Wet ingredients for kneaded bread
1 cup water

Wet ingredients for bread machines
1 cup + 2 tablespoons water

Steps for kneaded bread
Mix, knead, oil bowl
1st rise
Punch down, 2nd rise
Shape into braided circle
  (p. 20), 3rd rise
Crust: cornmeal and
  caraway seeds
Bake at 400° for 25–30
  minutes
Test for doneness and cool

Steps for bread machines
Put in bread machine to mix,
  knead, and rise
Remove from machine after
  2nd rise to finish by hand

Variation: Replace the bacon with breakfast sausage, browned and drained. You can also use cooked ham, beef, or any other meat. (The meat must be cooked and diced small.)

Crust: topping of cornmeal and caraway seeds
Prepare egg wash: Mix 1 beaten egg with 1 tablespoon milk or water. Before baking, brush with egg wash, sprinkle with sesame seeds, and brush again with egg wash. Then sprinkle with corn meal.

Braided Brioche

This is a buttery egg bread that can be braided, with a topping of seeds, or made with the traditional topknot. Make sure the liquids are at 120° and the other wet ingredients are warmed at least to room temperature. This bread is best served warm out of the oven. Cover any leftovers tightly, since the eggs will tend to dry out the bread.

Dry ingredients
3¼ cups bread flour
1 tablespoon yeast
  (2¼ teaspoons for bread
  machines)
2 tablespoons sugar
½ teaspoon salt

Wet ingredients for kneaded breads
¼ cup water (120°)
½ cup milk (120°)
½ cup very soft butter
3 eggs, beaten
1 egg yolk, beaten

Wet ingredients for bread machines
¼ cup + 2 tablespoons water
  (120°)
½ cup milk (120°)
½ cup very soft butter
3 eggs, beaten
1 egg yolk, beaten

Steps for kneaded bread

Mix (wet ingredients should be mixed with an electric mixer until creamy), knead, place in oiled bowl. 1st rise. Punch down, turn out on a lightly floured board, and knead lightly. For the topknot, cut off a piece of dough about the size of a golf ball. Shape remaining dough into a ball. Place in a greased 2-quart casserole bowl or brioche pan. Cut an X in the center of the ball with a sharp knife. Shape the small piece of dough into a teardrop shape, and place in the center of the X, point down. Cover and let rise until doubled in size, about 45 minutes to 1 hour. Crust: shiny. Bake at 375° for 30–35 minutes
Test for doneness and cool.

Steps for bread machines

Put in bread machine to mix, knead, and rise
Remove from machine after 1st rise to finish by hand

Variation: Braided Brioche: After 1st rise, shape into a braided circle (p. 00). 2nd rise (45 minutes to 1 hour). Crust: egg wash and seeds (your choice). Mix egg wash, as below, and sprinkle loaf with seeds before baking. Follow same baking directions as above.

Crust: shiny
Mix 1 beaten egg with 1 tablespoon milk or water. Before baking, brush loaf with egg wash.

Buccellati

This bread from northern Italy has the distinct taste of anise and a hint of lemon. Make sure that the liquids are at 120 degrees and that the other wet ingredients are warmed at least to room temperature.

Dry ingredients
3 cups bread flour
1 tablespoon yeast
   (2 ¼ teaspoons for bread machines)
2 ½ tablespoons anise seeds
2 tablespoons fresh lemon zest or finely minced lemon peel
3 tablespoons sugar
1 teaspoon salt

Wet ingredients for kneaded bread
¼ cup very soft butter
¼ cup port or Marsala wine (120°)
2 eggs, beaten
½ cup milk (120°)

Wet ingredients for bread machines
¼ cup very soft butter
¼ cup port or Marsala wine (120°)
2 eggs, beaten
½ cup + 3 tablespoons milk (120°)

Steps for kneaded bread
Mix (wet ingredients should be mixed with an electric mixer until creamy), knead, oil bowl. 1st rise. Punch down, knead lightly, and shape dough into a fat snake shape. Place on a sprayed baking sheet. Shape dough into a ring; pinch the ends together and tuck under, leaving a 4–5-inch hole in the middle. Cover and let rise about 1 hour, until doubled in size.
Crust: soft
Bake at 375° for 25–30 minutes
Test for doneness and cool

Steps for bread machines
Put in bread machine to mix, knead, and rise
Remove from machine after 1st rise to finish by hand

Crust: soft
Brush loaf with melted butter *after* baking.

Braided Greek Easter Bread

Dry ingredients
3 cups bread flour
1 tablespoon yeast
   (2¼ teaspoons for bread
   machines)
¼ cup sugar
1 teaspoon salt
1½ tablespoons lemon peel,
   minced
½ teaspoon anise

Wet ingredients for kneaded bread
½ cup milk
¼ cup butter, melted
3 eggs, beaten

Wet ingredients for bread machines
½ cup + 3 tablespoons milk
¼ cup butter, melted
3 eggs, beaten

Extra ingredient
4 unpeeled hard-boiled eggs,
dyed red (the traditional color)
or color of choice

Steps for kneaded bread
Mix, knead, oil bowl
1st rise
Punch down, shape into a
   round braid (p. 20). Tuck
   hard-boiled eggs securely into
   the folds of the braids around
   the top, bottom, and sides.
   Cover and let rise 1 hour.
Crust: shiny
Bake at 325⁰ for 45–50
   minutes
Test for doneness and cool

Steps for bread machines
Put in bread machine to mix,
   knead, and rise
Remove from machine after
   1st rise to finish by hand

Crust: shiny
Mix 1 beaten egg with 1 tablespoon milk
or water. Before baking, brush loaf with
egg wash.

Braided Jewish Challah

This bread traditionally calls for saffron, but even a "pinch" is pricey. Yellow food coloring will work.

Dry ingredients
3 cups bread flour
1 tablespoon yeast
   (2¼ teaspoons for bread
   machines)
½ teaspoon salt
1½ tablespoons sugar

Wet ingredients for kneaded bread
½ cup water
¼ cup butter, melted
2 eggs, beaten
Healthy pinch saffron, or 2–3
   drops yellow food coloring

Wet ingredients for bread machines
½ cup + 2 tablespoons water
¼ cup butter, melted
2 eggs, beaten
Healthy pinch saffron, or 2–3
   drops yellow food coloring

Steps for kneaded bread
Mix, knead, oil bowl
1st rise
Punch down, knead a few
   times, and shape into a braided circle (p. 20). Cover and
   let rise 1 hour.
Crust: sesame seeds
Bake at 350° for 30–35
   minutes
Test for doneness and cool

Steps for bread machines
Put in bread machine to mix,
   knead, and rise
Remove from machine after
   1st rise to finish by hand

Crust: topping of sesame seeds
Prepare egg wash: Mix 1 beaten egg with 1 tablespoon milk or water. Before baking, brush with egg wash, sprinkle with topping, and brush with egg wash again, using a patting motion.

IX
Artisan and Sourdough Breads

Every authority on artisan breads seems to have different preferences and methods—even different definitions of what an artisan bread is. The basic idea, at first, was to recreate rustic Old World–style peasant breads using only the ingredients that were traditionally available. Since commercial yeast was not available, all these breads relied on natural or "sourdough" starters. Many people now incorporate some commercial yeast into the starter, for more reliable results. Completely natural starters depend on the wild yeast in the air—and that in turn depends on conditions in your kitchen, and the wild yeast starter may need considerable attention to develop properly.

Artisan and other types of sourdough breads have a charm and character all their own. They have a nice open crumb and a chewy crust—plus the distinctive sourdough taste. The artisan breads typically use some whole grain flour, especially cracked wheat, and are usually shaped into round or oval loaves. There are various techniques for achieving this rustic bread, and all involve using starters. By carefully following the basic rules and guidelines in this chapter and picking the method that suits you best, you should be able to turn out a wonderful bread.

The basic recipes in this chapter can be adapted for any bread recipe in the book. The recipes are for one loaf. You may use an 8 x 4 inch pan or create a shape of your choice.

Starters have been made from many types of starchy ingredients, such as potatoes or milk. They can be made from any type of flour. Once you start having fun with these breads, you may want to experiment with other starter ingredients.

Starter recipes in this chapter are of three basic types: (1) natural starters made entirely from wild yeast, (2) starters created from commercial yeast, and (3) starters that are made with a small amount of commercial yeast in the starter and in the dry ingredients when making the bread. (For home baking I personally find the third method the most satisfying.) If you have been making a lot of bread recently, the air in your kitchen will be full of yeast spores, making it easier to create a natural starter. If you haven't made a starter before, though, it makes sense to begin with commercial yeast.

Except where a particular starter is specified, you can use whichever starter you prefer for bread recipes. You will notice that some of the sourdough bread recipes in this chapter call for commercial yeast in addition to starter.

EQUIPMENT YOU WILL NEED

A 1-quart container made of glass, crockery, or plastic. (Never use metal.) Make sure it is absolutely clean.

A wooden spoon (not metal).

A single layer of cheesecloth and a rubber band to keep the cheesecloth in place. It is a good idea to label the container.

BASIC STEPS IN MAKING AND MAINTAINING A STARTER

Mix the starter ingredients (pp. 176–179).

Let starter develop.

Feed (some starters need to be fed several times).

When starter is finished, add to wet ingredients of bread recipe.

Store remainder in refrigerator. It is advisable to feed starter once a week to maintain it.

Before using again, bring to room temperature.

My favorite place to grow starter is in my gas oven with just the pilot light going. it maintains a steady $80°$, which is perfect. (The starter will be in the oven for several days, and I flag the dial to the oven with a napkin so I don't forget and turn on the oven for something else.)

During the resting periods, stir the starter twice a day. If it becomes pinkish at any point, it has been spoiled by uninvited organisms, and you will need to discard it and begin again. Some starters need to be fed more and the steps are slightly different. Detailed steps are included in each starter recipe.

Natural Wheat Starter

This is called a "Friendship Starter": The idea is to make more than you need and pass the surplus on to a friend. A completely natural starter such as this requires more feeding and baby-sitting, because the wild yeast may take longer to grow.

Dry ingredients
3 cups all-purpose flour
   (unbleached)
½ cup whole wheat flour

Wet ingredients
⅓ cup grape or orange juice
2 cups water

Mix starter ingredients: Mix dry ingredients together. Bring wet ingredients to 115°. Mix wet and dry ingredients together until smooth.

Let starter grow: Place in the container and cover with one layer of cheesecloth, using a rubber band to secure. Let sit in a warm place for 12–24 hours, or until bubbles begin to form, stirring once or twice. If it turns a pinkish color, discard the starter and begin again.

Feed with 1 cup flour + 1 cup water, mixed together until smooth. Stir the mixture into the starter.

Let starter grow in a warm place for another 12 hours, or until bubbles form. Give ½ of the mixture to a friend (with feeding instructions). Feed twice more with ½ cup flour + ¼ cup water, and let develop for another 12 hours, stirring once or twice each time. Feed once more (½ cup flour + ¼ cup water), and let develop another 24 hours. It will be very bubbly and have a sour smell when it's ready.

First time use: Stir the starter until smooth and creamy, making sure it is at room temperature. Measure out the amount called for in the recipe.

Store and feed: Store what is not used in the fridge, covered with a tight-fitting lid. Feed once a week by stirring in ½ cup flour mixed with ¼ cup water. Let it sit out overnight and then refrigerate again.

Before using again: Take starter out of the refrigerator, give it a good stir, and leave it out overnight to reach room temperature.

Alaskan Sourdough Starter

Dry ingredients
2 cups all purpose flour
1 tablespoon sugar
1 teaspoon salt

Wet ingredients
2¼ cups warm water (115⁰)
2¼ teaspoons yeast, stirred
  into the water until dissolved

Mix starter ingredients: Mix dry ingredients together. Mix wet ingredients together and bring to 115⁰. Mix wet and dry ingredients together until smooth.

Let starter grow: Place in the container, cover with a single layer of cheesecloth, using a rubber band to secure. Store in a warm place for 3–5 days, or until the starter becomes bubbly and has a sour smell (the time may vary). Stir twice a day. The starter will smell like a brewery (this is good).

First time use: Stir the starter until smooth and creamy, making sure it is at room temperature. Measure out the amount called for in the recipe.

Store and feed (or replenish): Store what is not used in the fridge, covered with a tight-fitting lid. Feed once a week by stirring in ¼ cup flour and ¼ cup water (115⁰), mixed until smooth. Let it sit out overnight and then refrigerate again.

Before using again: Take starter out of the refrigerator, give it a good stir, and leave it out overnight to reach room temperature.

Rye Starter

Dry ingredients
½ cup rye flour
1 tablespoon caraway seeds,
crushed (crush them with the
bottom of a glass)

Wet ingredients
1 cup warm water (115⁰)
⅛ teaspoon yeast, stirred into
the water until dissolved
1 tablespoon minced onions

Mix starter ingredients: Mix
dry ingredients together. Mix
wet ingredients together and
bring to 115⁰. Mix wet and dry
ingredients together until
smooth.

Let starter grow: Place in the
container and cover with a
tight lid. Store in a warm place
for 24 hours. Stir twice during
that time.

Feed with 1 cup rye flour + ½
cup warm water, mixed until
smooth. Stir mixture into
starter. Let starter develop in a
warm place 24 hours more, or
until it has a sour smell.

First time use: Stir the starter
until smooth and creamy, making sure it is at room temperature. Measure out the amount
called for in the recipe.

Store and feed: Store what is
not used in the fridge, covered
with a tight-fitting lid. Feed once
a week by stirring in 1 cup rye
flour mixed with ½ cup warm
water. Let it sit out 24 hours
and then refrigerate again.

Before using again: Take
starter out of the refrigerator,
give it a good stir, and leave it
out overnight to reach room
temperature.

Beer Starter

Dry ingredients
1 cup unbleached all-purpose
  flour
¼ cup dried potato flakes
⅛ teaspoon salt

Wet ingredients
1¼ cups any kind of beer,
  warmed to 115°
⅛ teaspoon yeast, stirred into
  the water until dissolved

Mix starter ingredients: Mix
dry ingredients together with a
wire whisk, add the wet ingredients, and mix until smooth.

Let starter grow: Cover loosely
with a lid and let sit in a warm
place for 24 hours. Stir once.

Wet ingredients for feeding starter
¼ cup flour
¼ cup potato water
(Peel and dice 1 small potato,
  boil in 2 cups water, and
  mash in cooking water. If
  some of the water has boiled
  away, add enough water to
  equal 2 cups. Refrigerate the
  remaining potato water and
  use for feeding after using
  the starter.)

Feed with ¼ cup flour + ¼ cup

potato water, mixed until
smooth. Stir mixture into the
starter.

Let starter grow in a warm
place until it takes on a sour
smell. Stir once a day.

First time use: Stir the starter
until smooth and creamy, making sure it is at room temperature. Measure out the amount
called for in the recipe.

Store and feed: Store what is
not used in the fridge, covered
with a tight-fitting lid. Feed
once a week by stirring in ¼
cup flour mixed with ¼ cup
potato water (115°). Let it sit
out 24 hours and then refrigerate again.

Before using again: Take
starter out of the refrigerator,
give it a good stir, and leave it
out overnight to reach room
temperature.

Alaskan Sourdough Bread

Dry ingredients
3 cups bread flour
2 1/4 teaspoons yeast
1 teaspoon baking soda
1 teaspoon salt

Wet ingredients
1 cup Alaskan Sourdough
  Starter (p. 177)
1/2 cup warm water
1/4 cup butter, melted
1 large egg, lightly beaten

Steps for kneaded bread
Mix, knead, oil bowl
1st rise
Punch down, 2nd rise
Shape into a loaf of your
  choice, 3rd rise
Crust: chewy
Bake at 375° for 40 minutes
Test for doneness and cool

Crust: chewy
Steam the loaf: Place a pan on the floor of the oven. Preheat oven to full heat. Toss 6 to 8 ice cubes into the pan, place the loaf in right away, and close the door quickly.

Jewish Sour Onion Rye

Using onion and crushed caraway seeds in the starter is the secret to this fine bread.

Dry ingredients
2 cups bread flour
1 cup rye flour
2¼ teaspoons yeast
1 teaspoon salt
1 tablespoon caraway seeds
  (optional)

Wet ingredients
1 cup Rye Starter (p. 178)
½ cup water

Steps for kneaded bread
Mix, knead, oil bowl
1st rise
Punch down, 2nd rise
Shape into a loaf, 3rd rise
Crust: chewy, with caraway
  seeds
Bake at 375° for 25–30
  minutes
Test for doneness and cool

Crust: chewy, with caraway seeds
Prepare egg wash: Mix 1 beaten egg with 1 tablespoon milk or water. Before baking, brush with egg wash, sprinkle with caraway seeds, and brush with egg wash again, using a patting motion. Steam the loaf: Place a pan on the floor of the oven. Preheat oven to full heat. Toss 6 to 8 ice cubes into the pan and place the loaf in right away, and close the door quickly.

Whole Wheat Sourdough

A southwestern favorite

Dry ingredients

2 cups bread flour

1 cup whole wheat flour

½ teaspoon yeast

1 teaspoon salt

1 teaspoon ground cumin

Wet ingredients

1 cup starter (your choice, pp. 177–179)

½ cup warm water

Steps for kneaded bread

Mix, knead, oil bowl

1st rise

Punch down, 2nd rise

Shape (your choice, pp. 20–21), 3rd rise

Crust: very chewy

Bake at 400° for 25 minutes

Test for doneness and cool

Crust: very chewy

Prepare egg wash: Mix 1 beaten egg with 1 tablespoon milk or water. Before baking, brush with egg wash. Then steam: Place a pan on the floor of the oven. Preheat oven to full heat. Toss 6 to 8 ice cubes into the pan, place the loaf in right away, and close the door quickly.

Ksra

This Moroccan sourdough flatbread is usually served with olives and cheese. My husband David spent some time in Morocco and talks of this bread with great fondness.

Dry Ingredients

1 cup barley flour
1 cup whole wheat flour
1 teaspoon salt
2 teaspoons sugar

Wet Ingredients

2 cups starter (your choice, pp. 177–179)
½ cup milk
2 tablespoons melted butter

Steps for kneaded bread

Mix, knead, oil bowl
1st rise
Punch down, 2nd rise
Shape into a 10-inch flat circle, dust pan with cornmeal, 3rd rise
Crust: cornmeal
Bake at 375° for 25–30 minutes
Test for doneness and cool

Crust: topping of cornmeal
Prepare egg wash: Mix 1 beaten egg with 1 tablespoon milk or water. Before baking, brush with egg wash and sprinkle with topping.

Ciabatta

This is a traditional Italian flatbread made with a wet dough, which gives it its open crumb and chewy texture. One of my favorite breads!

Dry ingredients
3 cups bread flour
1½ teaspoons yeast
1½ teaspoons salt

Wet ingredients
½ cup Alaskan Sourdough
   Starter (p. 177)
⅔ cup warm water
½ cup + 2 tablespoons milk
½ tablespoon olive oil

Steps for kneaded bread
Mix, adding flour if needed,
   until the dough holds a
   shape; knead, oil bowl
1st rise
Punch down and knead only a
   few times, 2nd rise
Shape into a slipper shape, 3rd
   rise (about 30 minutes)
Crust: very chewy
Bake at 425° for 15 minutes.
   Turn oven to 375°, steam
   again, and bake another
   10–15 minutes.
Test for doneness and cool

Crust: very chewy
Prepare egg wash: Mix 1 beaten egg with 1 table-spoon milk or water. Before baking, brush with egg wash. Then steam: Place a pan on the floor of the oven. Preheat oven to full heat. Toss 6 to 8 ice cubes into the pan, place the loaf in right away, and close the door quickly. After 15 minutes, steam again, adding 6 to 8 more ice cubes.

Chocolate Sour Cherry
Sourdough Bread

This savory bread is delicious toasted, served with cream cheese and a good orange marmalade.

Special ingredient
1½ cups sour cherries, dried
Simmer cherries for 5 minutes in enough water to cover. Remove from heat, cool, and drain. Add to the dry ingredients.

Dry ingredients
3 cups bread flour
¼ teaspoon yeast
1 cup dark cocoa powder
1½ teaspoons salt
½ teaspoon white pepper

Wet ingredients
1 cup starter (your choice, pp. 177–179)
1 cup warm water

Steps for kneaded bread
Mix, knead, oil bowl
1st rise
Punch down, 2nd rise
Shape into a round loaf (p. 21), 3rd rise
Crust: chewy
Bake at 400° for 25–30 minutes
Test for doneness and cool

Crust: chewy
Steam the loaf: Place a pan on the floor of the oven. Preheat oven to full heat. Toss 6 to 8 ice cubes into the pan, place the loaf in right away, and close the door quickly.

Rosemary and Green Olive Sourdough Rye

Dry ingredients
2 cups bread flour
1 cup dark rye flour
1 teaspoon yeast
1 teaspoon salt
4 tablespoons fresh rosemary, coarsely chopped, or 3 tablespoons dried
¾ cup green salad olives, chopped small (including pimentos)

Wet ingredients
1 cup Beer Starter (p. 179)
1 cup potato water (p. 179)
¼ cup milk

Steps for kneaded bread
Mix, knead, oil bowl
1st rise
Punch down, 2nd rise
Shape (your choice, pp. 20–21), 3rd rise
Crust: chopped green olives
Bake at 400° for 25 minutes
Test for doneness and cool

Crust: topping of chopped green olives
Prepare egg wash: Mix 1 beaten egg with 1 tablespoon milk or water. Before baking, brush with egg wash, sprinkle with topping, and brush with egg wash again, using a patting motion.

X
A World of Bagels

The best bagels I have ever had were from a small bagel shop in Greenwich Village in New York City. Duplicating that chewy texture can be a challenge. Most cookbooks tell you to boil, broil, and then bake. After trying almost all combinations, I came up with the simplified method described in the next pages.

The recipe will make 6 bagels. If you want more bagels for your effort, simply double the recipe—after learning the basic method. It is my advice to try the recipe first and learn how the dough should feel. You can experiment with using other flours. Substituting ½ cup rye or whole wheat flour for a half cup of bread flour will give an interesting taste and texture to almost any bagel.

DETAILED STEPS FOR MAKING BAGELS

Mix: Mix the dry ingredients together. Mix the wet ingredients together (if needed), and heat to 120°. Mix until the dough leaves the sides of the bowl and is easy to handle. Add more flour or water if needed.

Knead: Knead until you have a smooth, elastic dough that springs back when pinched up (see instructions for kneading, p. 16).

Oil bowl, 1st rise: Oil your bowl and place the dough in the bowl. Turn the dough until all sides are coated with the oil. Let rise until doubled in bulk.

For bread machines: Put in bread machine to mix, knead, and rise. Remove to punch down and finish by hand. (See below.)

Punch down and cut into 3rds: Punch the dough down to deflate it and knead another few times. Divide into 3rds and make fat snakes with the dough.

Shape: Cut the snakes into 6 pieces. Roll them out further—but not too long, or you will end up with a large, flat bagel. Connect the ends by dabbing your fingers in water, wetting the ends, and pinching them closed (the water works to glue them together). Place bagels about 2 inches apart on a cookie sheet that has been well sprayed with cooking oil. Let rise 20–30 minutes. While the bagels are rising, boil 2 quarts of water, salted with 1 tablespoon of salt.

Boil: Place one bagel at a time in the boiling water and boil on each side for 1 minute. Place wet bagels back on the greased cookie sheet, and let them air dry. Preheat oven to 500°.

Topping: Prepare egg wash: Mix 1 beaten egg with 1 tablespoon milk or water. Using a pastry brush, coat bagels with egg wash. Sprinkle the wet bagel with the topping. With a patting motion, apply egg wash again, unless the topping is fine textured and would be washed off. The amount of topping is up to you. If you don't like the suggested topping, experiment with another topping of your choice.

Bake: Place a baking pan on the bottom rack of the oven. Place bagels in the oven on a sprayed cookie sheet. Pour 1 cup of ice water with 3 to 4 ice cubes into the baking pan. This will cause a burst of steam. Close the oven immediately, and bake for 10 minutes. Open the oven and take the bagels out. closing the oven right away. Turn the bagels over. Let the oven heat up for a few minutes, and place the bagels in the oven quickly. Add another cup of ice water with ice cubes, and close the oven door. Bake another 10 minutes or until golden brown. Remove from the oven and cool on a wire rack.

Basic Bagel Recipe

Dry ingredients
3 cups bread flour
1½ teaspoons yeast
  (same amount for bread
  machines)
1½ teaspoons salt
1 tablespoon sugar

**Wet ingredients for
kneaded bagels**
1 cup water

**Wet ingredients for
bread machines**
1 cup + 2 tablespoons water

Steps for kneaded bagels
Mix, knead, oil bowl
1st rise
Punch down and cut into thirds
Shape and boil
Add topping
Bake at 500° for 10 minutes,
  turn over, bake 10 minutes
  more, and cool

Steps for bread machines
Put in bread machine to mix,
  knead, and rise
Remove from machine to punch
  down and finish by hand

Sesame Bagels

Dry ingredients
3 cups bread flour
1½ teaspoons yeast
(same amount for bread
machines)
1½ teaspoons salt
1 tablespoon sugar
¼ cup toasted sesame seeds

Topping
2 tablespoons toasted
sesame seeds

Wet ingredients for kneaded bagels
1 cup water
1 tablespoon sesame oil

Wet ingredients for bread machines
1 cup + 2 tablespoons water
1 tablespoon sesame oil

Steps for kneaded bagels
Mix, knead, oil bowl
1st rise
Punch down and cut into thirds
Shape and boil
Add topping
Bake at 500° for 10 minutes,
turn over, bake 10 minutes
more, and cool

Steps for bread machines
Put in bread machine to mix,
knead, and rise
Remove from machine to
punch down and finish by
hand

Topping: sesame seeds
Prepare egg wash: Mix 1 beaten egg with 1 tablespoon milk or water. Before baking, brush with egg
wash, sprinkle with topping, and brush with egg
wash again, using a patting motion.

Lemon Pepper Bagels

Dry ingredients
3 cups bread flour
1½ teaspoons yeast
  (same amount for bread
  machines)
½ teaspoon salt
1 tablespoon sugar
1 tablespoon lemon pepper, or
  to taste

Topping
Lemon pepper

Wet ingredients for kneaded bagels
1 cup water

Wet ingredients for bread machines
1 cup + 2 tablespoons water

Steps for kneaded bagels
Mix, knead, oil bowl
1st rise
Punch down and cut into thirds
Shape and boil
Add topping
Bake at 500° for 10 minutes,
  turn over, bake 10 minutes
  more, and cool

Steps for bread machines
Put in bread machine to mix,
  knead, and rise
Remove from machine to
  punch down and finish by
  hand

Topping: lemon pepper
Prepare egg wash: Mix 1 beaten egg with 1 tablespoon milk or water. Before baking, brush with egg wash and sprinkle with topping.

Onion Bagels

Dry ingredients

3 cups bread flour

1½ teaspoons yeast
(same amount for bread
machines)

1½ teaspoons salt

1 tablespoon sugar

1 cup red onion, diced small,
sauteed with 1 tablespoon
butter, and drained (reserve
¼ cup for topping)

Topping

Reserved onion

Wet ingredients for kneaded bagels

1 cup water

Wet ingredients for bread machines

1 cup + 2 tablespoons water

Steps for kneaded bagels

Mix, knead, oil bowl

1st rise

Punch down and cut into thirds

Shape and boil

Add topping

Bake at 500° for 10 minutes,
turn over, bake 10 minutes
more, and cool

Steps for bread machines

Put in bread machine to mix,
knead, and rise

Remove from machine to
punch down and finish by
hand

Topping: sauteed onion
Prepare egg wash: Mix 1 beaten egg with
1 tablespoon milk or water. Before baking, brush
with egg wash, sprinkle with topping, and brush with
egg wash again, using a patting motion.

Onion Rye Bagels with Caraway Seeds

Dry ingredients
2 cups bread flour
1 cup dark rye flour
1½ teaspoons yeast
(same amount for bread
machines)
1½ teaspoons salt
1 tablespoon sugar
1 cup red onion, diced small,
sauteed with 1 tablespoon
butter, and drained
1 tablespoon caraway seeds

Topping
Caraway seeds

**Wet ingredients for
kneaded bagels**
1 cup water

**Wet ingredients for
bread machines**
1 cup + 2 tablespoons water

Steps for kneaded bagels
Mix, knead, oil bowl
1st rise
Punch down and cut into thirds
Shape and boil
Add topping
Bake at 500° for 10 minutes,
turn over, bake 10 minutes
more, and cool

Steps for bread machines
Put in bread machine to mix,
knead, and rise
Remove from machine to
punch down and finish by
hand

Topping: caraway seeds
Prepare egg wash: Mix 1 beaten egg with 1 tablespoon milk or water. Before baking, brush with egg
wash, sprinkle with topping, and brush with egg
wash again, using a patting motion.

Whole Wheat Bagels

Dry ingredients
2 cups bread flour
½ cup whole wheat bread flour
½ cup toasted wheat germ
1½ teaspoons yeast
  (same amount for bread
  machines)
1½ teaspoons salt
1 tablespoon sugar

Topping
Toasted wheat germ

**Wet ingredients for
kneaded bagels**
1 cup water

**Wet ingredients for
bread machines**
1 cup + 2 tablespoons water

Steps for kneaded bagels
Mix, knead, oil bowl
1st rise
Punch down and cut into thirds
Shape and boil
Add topping
Bake at 500⁰ for 10 minutes,
  turn over, bake 10 minutes
  more, and cool

Steps for bread machines
Put in bread machine to mix,
  knead, and rise
Remove from machine to
  punch down and finish by
  hand

Topping: toasted wheat germ
Prepare egg wash: Mix 1 beaten egg with 1
tablespoon milk or water. Before baking, brush
with egg wash and sprinkle with topping.

Four-Grain Bagels

Dry ingredients

2 cups bread flour

¼ cup each of rye, rice, buckwheat, and semolina flour

1½ teaspoons yeast
    (same amount for bread
    machines)

1½ teaspoons salt

1 tablespoon sugar

Topping

Sesame seeds

**Wet ingredients for
kneaded bagels**

1 cup water

**Wet ingredients for
bread machines**

1 cup + 2 tablespoons water

Steps for kneaded bagels

Mix, knead, oil bowl

1st rise

Punch down and cut into thirds

Shape and boil

Add topping

Bake at 500° for 10 minutes,
    turn over, bake 10 minutes
    more, and cool

Steps for bread machines

Put in bread machine to mix,
    knead, and rise

Remove from machine to
    punch down and finish by
    hand

Topping: sesame seeds
Prepare egg wash: Mix 1 beaten egg with 1 tablespoon milk or water. Before baking, brush with egg
wash, sprinkle with topping, and brush with egg
wash again, using a patting motion.

Pumpernickel Bagels

Dry ingredients
2 cups bread flour
1 cup pumpernickel (dark rye)
  flour
1½ teaspoons yeast
  (same amount for bread
  machines)
1½ teaspoons salt
1 tablespoon sugar
2 tablespoons caraway seeds
1 tablespoon instant coffee
  granules

Topping
Caraway seeds

Wet ingredients for kneaded bagels
1 cup water
2 tablespoons olive oil
2½ tablespoons molasses

Wet ingredients for bread machines
1 cup + 2 tablespoons water
2 tablespoons olive oil
2½ tablespoons molasses

Steps for kneaded bagels
Mix, knead, oil bowl
1st rise
Punch down and cut into thirds
Shape and boil
Add topping
Bake at 500° for 10 minutes,
  turn over, bake 10 minutes
  more, and cool

Steps for bread machines
Put in bread machine to mix,
  knead, and rise
Remove from machine to
  punch down and finish by
  hand

Topping: caraway seeds
Prepare egg wash: Mix 1 beaten egg with
1 tablespoon milk or water. Before baking,
brush with egg wash, sprinkle with topping,
and brush with egg wash again, using a
patting motion.

Green Olive Bagels

Dry ingredients
3 cups bread flour
1½ teaspoons yeast
(same amount for bread
machines)
1 teaspoon salt
1 tablespoon sugar
⅔ cup green olives stuffed with
pimento, chopped small
(reserve juice)

Topping
Green olive, chopped small

Wet ingredients for kneaded bagels
½ cup water
½ cup juice from olives

Wet ingredients for bread machines
½ cup + 2 tablespoons water
½ cup juice from olives

Steps for kneaded bagels
Mix, knead, oil bowl
1st rise
Punch down and cut into thirds
Shape and boil
Add topping
Bake at 500° for 10 minutes,
turn over, bake 10 minutes
more, and cool

Steps for bread machines
Put in bread machine to mix,
knead, and rise
Remove from machine to
punch down and finish by
hand

Topping: chopped green olives
Prepare egg wash: Mix 1 beaten egg with
1 tablespoon milk or water. Before baking, brush
with egg wash, sprinkle with topping, and brush with
egg wash again, using a patting motion.

Cheddar Herb Bagels

Dry ingredients
2½ cups bread flour
½ cup rye flour (light or dark)
1½ teaspoons yeast
  (same amount for bread
  machines)
1½ teaspoons salt
1 tablespoon sugar
1 cup mild cheddar cheese,
  shredded
1 tablespoon each fresh basil,
  cilantro, parsley, oregano,
  and celery leaves, coarsely
  chopped and packed

Topping
Sesame and poppy seeds

Wet ingredients for kneaded bagels
1 cup water

Wet ingredients for bread machine
1 cup + 2 tablespoons water

Steps for kneaded bagels
Mix, knead, oil bowl
1st rise
Punch down and cut into thirds
Shape and boil
Add topping
Bake at 500° for 10 minutes,
  turn over, bake 10 minutes
  more, and cool

Steps for bread machines
Put in bread machine to mix,
  knead, and rise
Remove from machine to
  punch down and finish by
  hand

Topping: sesame and poppy seeds
Prepare egg wash: Mix 1 beaten egg with 1 tablespoon milk or water. Before baking, brush with egg wash, sprinkle with topping, and brush with egg wash again, using a patting motion.

Thyme and Cheese Bagels

Dry ingredients
3 cups bread flour
1½ teaspoons yeast
  (same amount for bread
  machines)
1½ teaspoons salt
1 tablespoon sugar
3 tablespoons fresh thyme,
  coarsely chopped and packed
1 cup Monterey Jack cheese,
  grated

Topping
Monterey Jack cheese, grated

Wet ingredients for kneaded bagels
1 cup water

Wet ingredients for bread machines
1 cup + 2 tablespoons water

Steps for kneaded bagels
Mix, knead, oil bowl
1st rise
Punch down and cut into thirds
Shape and boil
Topping: grated Monterey Jack
  cheese
Bake at 500° for 10 minutes,
  turn over, bake 10 minutes
  more, and cool

Steps for bread machines
Put in bread machine to mix,
  knead, and rise
Remove from machine to
  punch down and finish by
  hand

Topping: grated Monterey Jack cheese
Sprinkle thinly on bagels during last 5
minutes of baking, or just long enough to
melt and become chewy slightly

Mozzarella Dill Bagels

Dry ingredients
2½ cups bread flour
½ cup whole wheat flour
1½ teaspoons yeast
  (same amount for bread
  machines)
1½ teaspoons salt
1 tablespoon sugar
1 cup mozzarella cheese,
  shredded
2 tablespoons dill weed, dried,
  or 3 tablespoons fresh

Topping
Mozzarella cheese, shredded

Wet ingredients for kneaded bagels
1 cup water

Wet ingredients for bread machines
1 cup + 2 tablespoons water

Steps for kneaded bagels
Mix, knead, oil bowl
1st rise
Punch down and cut into thirds
Shape and boil
Topping: shredded Mozzarella
  cheese
Bake at 500° for 10 minutes,
  turn over, bake 10 minutes
  more, and cool

Steps for bread machines
Put in bread machine to mix,
  knead, and rise
Remove from machine to
  punch down and finish by
  hand

Topping: shredded Mozzarella cheese
Sprinkle thinly on bagels during last 5
minutes of baking, or just long enough to
melt and become chewy slightly

Bacon Cheddar Bagels

Dry ingredients

3 cups bread flour

$1\frac{1}{2}$ teaspoons yeast
(same amount for bread
machines)

$1\frac{1}{2}$ teaspoons salt

1 tablespoon sugar

1 cup bacon, diced, fried, and
drained

1 cup mild cheddar cheese,
coarsely grated

Topping

Cheddar cheese, coarsely
grated

**Wet ingredients for
kneaded bagels**

1 cup water

**Wet ingredients for
bread machines**

1 cup + 2 tablespoons water

Steps for kneaded bagels

Mix, knead, oil bowl

1st rise

Punch down and cut into thirds

Shape and boil

Topping: grated cheddar
cheese

Bake at 500° for 10 minutes,
turn over, bake 10 minutes
more and cool

Steps for bread machines

Put in bread machine to mix,
knead, and rise

Remove from machine to
punch down and finish by
hand

Topping: grated cheddar cheese
Sprinkle thinly on bagels during last 5
minutes of baking, or just long enough to
melt and become chewy slightly

Cilantro Smoked-Cheese Bagels

Dry ingredients
3 cups bread flour
1½ teaspoons yeast
(same amount for bread
machines)
1½ teaspoons salt
1 tablespoon sugar
1 cup fresh cilantro, coarsely
chopped and loosely packed
1 cup smoked cheese,
shredded

Topping
Smoked cheese

Wet ingredients for kneaded bagels
1 cup water

Wet ingredients for bread machine bagels
1 cup + 2 tablespoons water

Steps for kneaded bagels
Mix, knead, oil bowl
1st rise
Punch down and cut into thirds
Shape and boil
Topping: shredded smoked
cheese
Bake at 500° for 10 minutes,
turn over, bake 10 minutes
more, and cool

Steps for bread machines
Put in bread machine to mix,
knead, and rise
Remove from machine to
punch down and finish by
hand

Topping: shredded smoked cheese
Sprinkle thinly on bagels during last 5
minutes of baking, or just long enough to
melt and become chewy slightly

Garlic Parmesan Bagels

Dry ingredients
2½ cups bread flour
½ cup rye flour
1½ teaspoons yeast
   (same amount for bread
   machines)
1½ teaspoons salt
1 tablespoon sugar
1 cup fresh Parmesan cheese,
   grated, or mozzarella cheese,
   shredded
2 tablespoons minced garlic, or
   to taste

Topping
Parmesan cheese

**Wet ingredients for
kneaded bagels**
1 cup water

**Wet ingredients for
bread machines**
1 cup + 2 tablespoons water

Steps for kneaded bagels
Mix, knead, oil bowl
1st rise
Punch down and cut into thirds
Shape and boil
Add topping
Bake at 500° for 10 minutes,
   turn over, bake 10 minutes
   more, and cool

Steps for bread machines
Put in bread machine to mix,
   knead, and rise
Remove from machine to
   punch down and finish by
   hand

Topping: Parmesan cheese
Prepare egg wash: Mix 1 beaten egg with 1
tablespoon milk or water. Before baking, brush
with egg wash and sprinkle with topping.

Sun-Dried Tomato and Cheese Bagel

Dry ingredients
3 cups bread flour
1½ teaspoons yeast
  (same amount for bread
  machines)
1½ teaspoons salt
1 tablespoon sugar
1 cup mozzarella cheese,
  shredded
1 cup sun-dried tomatoes,
  diced small

Topping
Sun-dried tomato bits (optional)

**Wet ingredients for
kneaded bagels**
1 cup water

**Wet ingredients for
bread machines**
1 cup + 2 tablespoons water

Steps for kneaded bagels
Mix, knead, oil bowl
1st rise
Punch down and cut into thirds
Shape and boil
Add topping
Bake at 500° for 10 minutes,
  turn over, bake 10 minutes
  more, and cool

Steps for bread machines
Put in bread machine to mix,
  knead, and rise
Remove from machine to
  punch down, and finish by
  hand

Topping: sun-dried tomato bits
Prepare egg wash: Mix 1 beaten egg with
1 tablespoon milk or water. Before baking, brush
with egg wash, sprinkle with topping, and brush with
egg wash again, using a patting motion.

Basil Tomato Bagels

Dry ingredients
3 cups bread flour
1½ teaspoons yeast
  (same amount for bread
  machines)
1½ teaspoons salt
1 tablespoon sugar
⅔ cup fresh basil, chopped
  small and packed

Topping
Poppy seeds

Wet ingredients for kneaded bagels
1 cup minus ½ tablespoon
  water
1 tablespoon tomato paste

Wet ingredients for bread machines
1 cup + 1½ tablespoons water
1 tablespoon tomato paste

Steps for kneaded bagels
Mix, knead, oil bowl
1st rise
Punch down and cut into thirds
Shape and boil
Add topping
Bake at 500° for 10 minutes,
  turn over, bake 10 minutes
  more, and cool

Steps for bread machines
Put in bread machine to mix,
  knead, and rise
Remove from machine to
  punch down and finish by
  hand

Topping: poppy seeds
Prepare egg wash: Mix 1 beaten egg with 1 tablespoon milk or water. Before baking, brush with egg
wash, sprinkle with topping, and brush with egg
wash again, using a patting motion.

Spinach Bagels

Dry ingredients
3 cups bread flour
1½ teaspoons yeast
   (same amount for bread
   machines)
1½ teaspoons salt
1 tablespoon sugar
⅛ teaspoon ground nutmeg
   (optional)

Topping
Sesame seeds

Wet ingredients for kneaded bagels
1 cup water
1 cup fresh spinach, chopped
   small and packed

Wet ingredients for bread machines
1 cup + 2 tablespoons water
1 cup fresh spinach, chopped
   small and packed

Steps for kneaded bagels
Mix, knead, oil bowl
1st rise
Punch down and cut into thirds
Shape and boil
Add topping
Bake at 500° for 10 minutes,
   turn over, bake 10 minutes
   more, and cool

Steps for bread machines
Put in bread machine to mix,
   knead, and rise
Remove to punch down and
   finish by hand

Topping: sesame seeds
Prepare egg wash: Mix 1 beaten egg with 1 tablespoon milk or water. Before baking, brush with egg wash, sprinkle with topping, and brush with egg wash again, using a patting motion.

Pesto Bagels

Dry ingredients
3 cups bread flour
$1\frac{1}{2}$ teaspoons yeast
  (same amount for bread
  machines)
$1\frac{1}{2}$ teaspoons salt
1 tablespoon sugar
1 tablespoon sesame seeds

Topping
Toasted sesame seeds

Wet ingredients for kneaded bagels
1 cup pesto sauce
Water, 1 tablespoon at a time,
  as needed

Wet ingredients for bread machines
1 cup pesto sauce
2 tablespoons water, or as
  required

Steps for kneaded bagels
Mix, knead, oil bowl
1st rise
Punch down, and cut into
  thirds
Shape and boil
Add topping
Bake at $500°$ for 10 minutes,
  turn over, bake 10 minutes
  more, and cool

Steps for bread machines
Put in bread machine to mix,
  knead, and rise
Remove to punch down, and
  finish by hand

Topping: toasted sesame seeds
Prepare egg wash: Mix 1 beaten egg with 1 tablespoon milk or water. Before baking, brush with egg
wash, sprinkle with topping, and brush with egg
wash again, using a patting motion.

Chili Bagels

Dry ingredients
3 cups bread flour
1½ teaspoons yeast
  (same amount for bread
  machines)
1½ teaspoons salt
1 tablespoon sugar

Wet ingredients for kneaded bagels
1 cup thick, cold chili, mashed
Up to ¾ cup water, ¼ cup at a
  time, as needed

Wet ingredients for bread machines
1 cup thick, cold chili, mashed
Up to 1⅛ cups water, or as
  required

Steps for kneaded bagels
Mix, knead, oil bowl
1st rise
Punch down and cut into thirds
Shape and boil
Add topping
Bake at 500° for 10 minutes,
  turn over, bake 10 minutes
  more, and cool

Steps for bread machines
Put in bread machine to mix,
  knead, and rise
Remove from machine to
  punch down and finish by
  hand

Topping: poppy seeds
Prepare egg wash: Mix 1 beaten egg with 1 tablespoon milk or water. Before baking, brush with egg
wash, sprinkle with topping, and brush with egg
wash again, using a patting motion.

Salsa Bagels

Dry ingredients
3 cups bread flour
1½ teaspoons yeast
  (same amount for bread
  machines)
1½ teaspoons salt
1 tablespoon sugar

Wet ingredients for kneaded bagels
1¼ cups salsa, or as needed

Wet ingredients for bread machines
2 tablespoons water
1¼ cups salsa, or as needed

Steps for kneaded bagels
Mix, knead, oil bowl
1st rise
Punch down and cut into thirds
Shape and boil
Add topping
Bake at 500° for 10 minutes,
  turn over, bake 10 minutes
  more, and cool

Steps for bread machines
Put in bread machine to mix,
  knead, and rise
Remove from machine to
  punch down and finish by
  hand

Crust: chewy
Steam the loaf: Place a pan on the floor of the oven. Preheat oven to full heat. Toss 6 to 8 ice cubes into the pan, place the loaf in right away, and close the door quickly.

Red Hot Bagels

Dry ingredients
3 cups bread flour
1½ teaspoons yeast
(same amount for bread machines)
1½ teaspoons salt
1 tablespoon sugar
2–3 tablespoons crushed red chile peppers, or to taste

Topping
Crushed red chile peppers

Wet ingredients for kneaded bagels
1 cup water
2 teaspoons to 1 tablespoon liquid cayenne pepper

Wet ingredients for bread machines
1 cup + 2 tablespoons water
2 teaspoons to 1 tablespoon liquid cayenne pepper

Steps for kneaded bagels
Mix, knead, oil bowl
1st rise
Punch down and cut into thirds
Shape and boil
Add topping
Bake at 500° for 10 minutes, turn over, bake 10 minutes more, and cool

Steps for bread machines
Put in bread machine to mix, knead, and rise
Remove from machine to punch down and finish by hand

Topping: crushed red chile peppers
Prepare egg wash: Mix 1 beaten egg with 1 tablespoon milk or water. Before baking, brush with egg wash, sprinkle with topping, and brush with egg wash again, using a patting motion.

Savory Bagel Variations

Type of Bagel	Add to dry ingredients	Add to wet ingredients	Toppings
Anise Seed Bagels	3 tablespoons anise seeds, crushed		
Coarse Salt Bagels			coarse salt
Caraway Seed Bagels	2 tablespoons caraway seeds		
Garlic Bagels		3 tablespoons garlic, minced	garlic, minced
Poppy Seed Bagels	3 tablespoons poppy seeds		poppy seeds
Cumin Seed Bagels	3 tablespoons cumin seeds, crushed		cumin seeds, crushed
Roasted Pumpkin Seed Bagels	1 cup roasted pumpkin seeds, coarsely chopped		pumpkin seeds
Fresh Ginger Bagels	4 tablespoons fresh ginger, grated		

SWEET BAGELS
Raspberry Bagels

Dry ingredients

3 cups bread flour

1½ teaspoons yeast
(same amount for bread
machines)

1½ teaspoons salt

3 tablespoons sugar

1 cup fresh raspberries

**Wet ingredients for
kneaded bagels**

1 cup water

**Wet ingredients for
bread machines**

1 cup + 2 tablespoons water

Steps for kneaded bagels

Mix, knead, oil bowl

1st rise

Punch down and cut into thirds

Shape and boil

Bake at 500° for 10 minutes,
turn over, bake 10 minutes
more, and cool

Steps for bread machines

Put in bread machine to mix,
knead, and rise

Remove from machine to
punch down and finish by
hand

Variation 1: Blueberry
Bagels. Substitute 1 cup
fresh blueberries for the
raspberries.

Variation 2: Strawberry
Banana Bagels. Substitute
½ cup fresh strawberries
for the raspberries. Add ½
cup mashed bananas to
wet ingredients.

Honey Wheat Bagels

Dry ingredients
2 cups bread flour
1 cup whole wheat bread flour
1½ teaspoons yeast
(same amount for bread
machines)
1½ teaspoons salt

**Wet ingredients for
kneaded bagels**
¾ cup water
⅔ cup honey

**Wet ingredients for
bread machines**
¾ cup + 2 tablespoons water
⅔ cup honey

Steps for kneaded bagels
Mix, knead, oil bowl
1st rise
Punch down and cut into thirds
Shape and boil
Bake at 500° for 10 minutes,
turn over, bake 10 minutes
more, and cool

Steps for bread machines
Put in bread machine to mix,
knead, and rise
Remove from machine to
punch down and finish by
hand

Chocolate Chip Bagels

Dry ingredients
3 cups bread flour
1½ teaspoons yeast
   (same amount for bread
   machines)
1½ teaspoons salt
3 tablespoons sugar
1 cup chocolate chips

**Wet ingredients for
kneaded bagels**
¾ cup water
⅔ cup honey

**Wet ingredients for
bread machines**
¾ cup + 2 tablespoons water
⅔ cup honey

Steps for kneaded bagels
Mix, knead, oil bowl
1st rise
Punch down and cut into thirds
Shape and boil
Bake at 500° for 10 minutes,
   turn over, bake 10 minutes
   more, and cool

Steps for bread machines
Put in bread machine to mix,
   knead, and rise
Remove from machine to
   punch down and finish by
   hand

Toasted Almond Bagels

Dry ingredients

3 cups bread flour

1½ teaspoons yeast
  (same amount for bread
  machines)

1½ teaspoons salt

3 tablespoon sugar

1 cup almond slivers, toasted
  and coarsly chopped

**Wet ingredients for
kneaded bagels**

1 cup water

1 teaspoon almond extract

**Wet ingredients for
bread machines**

1 cup + 2 tablespoons water

1 teaspoon almond extract

Steps for kneaded bagels

Mix, knead, oil bowl

1st rise

Punch down and cut into thirds

Shape and boil

Bake at 500° for 10 minutes,
  turn over, bake 10 minutes
  more, and cool

Steps for bread machines

Put in bread machine to mix,
  knead, and rise

Remove from machine to
  punch down and finish by
  hand

Date Walnut Bagels

Dry ingredients
3 cups bread flour
1½ teaspoons yeast
(same amount for bread
machines)
1½ teaspoons salt
1 tablespoon sugar
1 cup dried dates,
chopped small
½ cup walnuts, chopped small

**Wet ingredients for
kneaded bagels**
1 cup pineapple juice

**Wet ingredients for
bread machines**
1 cup + 2 tablespoons
pineapple juice

Steps for kneaded bagels
Mix, knead, oil bowl
1st rise
Punch down and cut into thirds
Shape and boil
Bake at 500° for 10 minutes,
turn over, bake 10 minutes
more, and cool

Steps for bread machines
Put in bread machine to mix,
knead, and rise
Remove from machine to
punch down and finish by
hand

Orange Marmalade
Toasted-Coconut Bagels

Dry ingredients

3 cups bread flour

1½ teaspoons yeast
  (same amount for bread
  machines)

1½ teaspoons salt

1 tablespoon sugar

1 cup toasted coconut, finely
  shredded

Wet ingredients for
kneaded bagels

1 cup orange marmalade

Water, as needed, 1 tablespoon
  at a time

Wet ingredients for
bread machines

1 cup orange marmalade

Water, as needed, 1 tablespoon
  at a time

Steps for kneaded bagels

Mix, knead, oil bowl

1st rise

Punch down and cut into thirds

Shape and boil

Bake at 500° for 10 minutes,
  turn over, bake 10 minutes
  more, and cool

Steps for bread machines

Put in bread machine to mix,
  knead, and rise

Remove from machine to
  punch down and finish by
  hand

Sour Cherry Bagels

Dry ingredients
3 cups bread flour
1½ teaspoons yeast
  (same amount for bread
  machines)
1½ teaspoons salt
1 tablespoon sugar

Wet ingredients for kneaded bagels
1 cup sour cherry pie filling
Water, as needed, 1 tablespoon
  at a time

Wet ingredients for bread machines
1 cup sour cherry pie filling
Water, as needed, 1 tablespoon
  at a time

Steps for kneaded bagels
Mix, knead, oil bowl
1st rise
Punch down and cut into thirds
Shape and boil
Bake at 500^0 for 10 minutes,
  turn over, bake 10 minutes
  more, and cool

Steps for bread machines
Put in bread machine to mix,
  knead, and rise
Remove from machine to
  punch down and finish by
  hand

Apple Spice Bagels

Dry ingredients

3 cups bread flour

$1\frac{1}{2}$ teaspoons yeast
(same amount for bread
machines)

$1\frac{1}{2}$ teaspoons salt

1 tablespoon sugar

1 cup Granny Smith apples,
peeled and diced small

1 tablespoon allspice

Wet ingredients for kneaded bagels

1 cup apple juice

Wet ingredients for bread machines

1 cup + 2 tablespoons
apple juice

Steps for kneaded bagels

Mix, knead, oil bowl

1st rise

Punch down and cut into thirds

Shape and boil

Bake at $500°$ for 10 minutes,
turn over, bake 10 minutes
more, and cool

Steps for bread machines

Put in bread machine to mix,
knead, and rise

Remove from machine to
punch down and finish by
hand

Pumpkin Pie Bagels

Dry ingredients
3 cups bread flour
1½ teaspoons yeast
  (same amount for bread
  machines)
1½ teaspoons salt
3 tablespoons sugar
2 teaspoons pumpkin spice, or
  to taste

**Wet ingredients for
kneaded bagels**
1 cup canned pumpkin
Water, 1 tablespoon at a time
  or as needed

**Wet ingredients for
bread machines**
1 cup canned pumpkin
Water, 1 tablespoon at a time
  as required

Steps for kneaded bagels
Mix, knead, oil bowl
1st rise
Punch down and cut into thirds
Shape and boil
Add topping
Bake at 500° for 10 minutes,
  turn over, bake 10 minutes
  more

**Steps for bread
machine bagels**
Put in bread machine to mix,
  knead, and rise
Remove from machine to
  punch down and finish by
  hand

Topping: pumpkin seeds, chopped
Prepare egg wash: Mix 1 beaten egg with 1 tablespoon milk or water. Before baking, brush with egg
wash, sprinkle with topping, and brush with egg
wash again, using a patting motion.

XI
Focaccia, Pizza, and Other Flatbreads

The basic recipe for Focaccia and Pizza that I use is Nanny Pezzaniti's. My grandmother made these wonderful foods often, and they are high on my list of favorites. Not only are they delicious but they offer endless possibilities for toppings. The toppings for focaccia can be simple or elaborate. I suggest trying a few recipes that appeal to you, and then experiment with topping combinations of your own. Like pizza, focaccia can be a meal in itself. The bread layer for focaccia is thicker, but you can heap the top with hearty combinations of cheese, meat, and vegetables.

For some breads I've indicated that you could leave out the oil, but for focaccia I strongly recommend that you use the full amount for a good texture. Experts are saying that olive oil, which is high in monounsaturates, is very good for you.

DETAILED STEPS FOR MAKING FOCACCIA

(Topping ingredients and instructions are listed in the recipes)

Mix: Mix all the dry ingredients together with a wire whisk. Mix the wet ingredients together (if needed) and add to the dry ingredients. Mix until the dough leaves the side of the bowl, adding more water or flour as needed.

Knead: Knead until soft and elastic (see instructions for kneading, p. 16).

Oil bowl: Oil your bowl by rubbing all sides generously with oil. Place the dough in the bowl, turning to coat all sides with oil.

1st rise: Let rise in a warm spot until doubled in size.

Punch down, shape, 2nd rise: Punch down to deflate. Divide the dough in half, or leave whole for a large focaccia. Roll out with a rolling pin or shape with the palms of your hands into a round or loaf shape about $1\frac{1}{2}$ inches thick. Place on a cookie sheet or pizza pan sprayed with cooking spray or coated with vegetable oil and let rise 20–30 minutes.

Prepare topping during 2nd rise.

Prepare for baking: Preheat oven to 500^0. Make small dimples in the dough with your fingertips (to keep it from bubbling). Brush the center of the dough with olive oil, leaving an inch all around..

Add topping and egg wash: Center the toppings, leaving about 1 inch around the outside for the crust. Add cheese first, then veggies, and finally meat—in that order. (If cheese is added last, it can make the focaccia soggy.) Prepare egg wash (optional): Mix 1 beaten egg with 1 tablespoon milk or water. Brush the outside crust (not the topping) with egg wash for a chewy texture. Add seeds for extra texture and brush with egg wash again (optional).

Bake: Bake for 20–25 minutes, or until golden brown, and serve.

Basic Focaccia Recipe

Topping of your choice

Dry ingredients
3 cups bread flour
2¼ teaspoons yeast
  (same amount for bread
  machines)
1½ teaspoons salt

**Wet ingredients for
kneaded bread**
¾ cup water
¼ cup olive oil

**Wet ingredients for
bread machines**
¾ cup + 2 tablespoons water
¼ cup olive oil

Steps for kneaded bread
Mix, knead, oil bowl
1st rise
Punch down, shape, 2nd rise
Prepare topping
Add topping and egg wash
Bake at 500° for 20–25
  minutes

Steps for bread machines
Put in bread machine to mix,
  knead, and rise
Remove dough after 1st rise to
  finish by hand

Onion Potato Focaccia with Mustard and Dill

Topping
1 cup each onion and unpeeled
   potato, very thinly sliced
1–2 tablespoons olive oil
Fresh dill
Salt and pepper to taste
Toss onion and potato with
   olive oil and sprinkle with
   salt, pepper, and dill weed.
   Spread evenly on a cookie
   sheet or sheet pan and bake
   at 400° until just tender.
   Spread evenly on focaccia
   dough and bake.

Dry ingredients
3 cups bread flour
2¼ teaspoons yeast
   (same amount for bread
   machines)
1½ teaspoons salt
3 tablespoons dried dill weed

Wet ingredients for kneaded bread
¾ cup water
¼ cup olive oil
3 tablespoons mustard

Wet ingredients for bread machines
¾ cup + 2 tablespoons water
¼ cup olive oil
3 tablespoons mustard

Steps for kneaded bread
Mix, knead, oil bowl
1st rise
Punch down, shape, 2nd rise
Prepare topping
Add topping and egg wash
Bake at 500° for 20–25
   minutes

Steps for bread machines
Put in bread machine to mix,
   knead, and rise
Remove dough after 1st rise to
   finish by hand

Spinach Focaccia with Smoked Cheese

Topping
1½ cups smoked cheese
1 cup fresh spinach, chopped
small, blanched, and dried
with paper towels

Dry ingredients
3 cups bread flour
2¼ teaspoons yeast
(same amount for bread
machines)
1½ teaspoons salt

**Wet ingredients for
kneaded bread**
¾ cup water
¼ cup olive oil
1 cup fresh spinach,
chopped small

**Wet ingredients for
bread machines**
¾ cup + 2 tablespoons water
¼ cup olive oil
1 cup fresh spinach,
chopped small

Steps for kneaded bread
Mix, knead, oil bowl
1st rise
Punch down, shape, 2nd rise
Prepare topping
Add topping and egg wash
Bake at 500° for 20–25
minutes

Steps for bread machines
Put in bread machine to mix,
knead, and rise
Remove dough after 1st rise to
finish by hand

Parmesan Focaccia with Seeds and Green Onons

Topping
2 tablespoons each sesame, poppy, sunflower, and pumpkin seeds
1 cup green onion, thinly sliced and packed
½ cup Parmesan cheese sprinkled over the top

Dry ingredients
3 cups bread flour
2¼ teaspoons yeast (same amount for bread machines)
1½ teaspoons salt
½ cup fresh Parmesan cheese, shredded

Wet ingredients for kneaded bread
¾ cup water
¼ cup olive oil

Wet ingredients for bread machines
¾ cup + 2 tablespoons water
¼ cup olive oil

Steps for kneaded bread
Mix, knead, oil bowl, 1st rise
Punch down, shape, 2nd rise
Prepare topping
Add topping and egg wash
Bake at 500° for 20–25 minutes

Steps for bread machines
Put in bread machine to mix, knead, and rise
Remove dough after 1st rise to finish by hand

Basil Garlic Focaccia

Topping

1 cup fresh basil, coarsely
chopped
3 tablespoons garlic, or to
taste, minced

Dry ingredients

3 cups bread flour
2¼ teaspoons yeast
(same amount for bread
machines)
1½ teaspoons salt
3 tablespoons dried basil flakes

**Wet ingredients for
kneaded bread**

¾ cup water
¼ cup olive oil

**Wet ingredients for
bread machines**

¾ cup + 2 tablespoons water
¼ cup olive oil

Steps for kneaded bread

Mix, knead, oil bowl
1st rise
Punch down, shape, 2nd rise
Prepare topping
Add topping and egg wash
Bake at 500° for 20–25
minutes

Steps for bread machines

Put in bread machine to mix,
knead, and rise
Remove dough after 1st rise to
finish by hand

Prosciutto Tomato Focaccia with Garlic

Prepare topping
2 cups prosciutto, very thinly
  sliced and diced
2 large tomatoes, thinly sliced
  and drained on paper towels

Dry ingredients
3 cups bread flour
2¼ teaspoons yeast
  (same amount for bread
  machines)
1½ teaspoons salt
3 tablespoons garlic, or to
  taste, minced

**Wet ingredients for
kneaded bread**
¾ cup water
¼ cup olive oil

**Wet ingredients for
bread machines**
¾ cup + 2 tablespoons water
¼ cup olive oil

Steps for kneaded bread
Mix, knead, oil bowl
1st rise
Punch down, shape, 2nd rise
Prepare topping
Add topping and egg wash
Bake at 500° for 20–25
  minutes

Steps for bread machines
Put in bread machine to mix,
  knead, and rise
Remove dough after 1st rise to
  finish by hand

Garlic Pepper Focaccia

Topping
3 tablespoons garlic, or to
   taste, minced
Freshly ground black pepper
   to taste

Dry ingredients
3 cups bread flour
2 $\frac{1}{4}$ teaspoons yeast
   (same amount for bread
   machines)
1 $\frac{1}{2}$ teaspoons salt
$\frac{1}{2}$ tablespoon black pepper,
   freshly ground

Wet ingredients for
kneaded bread
$\frac{3}{4}$ cup water
$\frac{1}{4}$ cup olive oil

Wet ingredients for
bread machines
$\frac{3}{4}$ cup + 2 tablespoons water
$\frac{1}{4}$ cup olive oil

Steps for kneaded bread
Mix, knead, oil bowl
1st rise
Punch down, shape, 2nd rise
Prepare topping
Add topping and egg wash
Bake at 500° for 20–25
   minutes

Steps for bread machines
Put in bread machine to mix,
   knead, and rise
Remove dough after 1st rise to
   finish by hand

Anchovy Focaccia with Green Onion

Topping
Anchovies to taste, coarsely
  chopped
1 cup green onion, tops only,
  thinly sliced

Dry ingredients
3 cups bread flour
$2\frac{1}{4}$ teaspoons yeast
  (same amount for bread
  machines)
$1\frac{1}{2}$ teaspoons salt

Wet ingredients for kneaded bread
$\frac{3}{4}$ cup water
$\frac{1}{4}$ cup olive oil
1 tablespoon anchovy paste
  (optional)

Wet ingredients for bread machines
$\frac{3}{4}$ cup + 2 tablespoons water
$\frac{1}{4}$ cup olive oil
1 tablespoon anchovy paste
  (optional)

Steps for kneaded bread
Mix, knead, oil bowl
1st rise
Punch down, shape, 2nd rise
Prepare topping
Add topping and egg wash
Bake at 500° for 20–25
  minutes

Steps for bread machines
Put in bread machine to mix,
  knead, and rise
Remove dough after 1st rise to
  finish by hand

Sun-Dried Tomato and Onion Focaccia

Topping

2 cups sun-dried tomatoes,
chopped small, soaked in hot
water 15–20 minutes,
drained and patted dry

1 cup red onion, diced small

Dry ingredients

3 cups bread flour

2$\frac{1}{4}$ teaspoons yeast
(same amount for bread
machines)

1$\frac{1}{2}$ teaspoons salt

1 tablespoon onion powder

**Wet ingredients for
kneaded bread**

$\frac{3}{4}$ cup water

$\frac{1}{4}$ cup olive oil

**Wet ingredients for
bread machines**

$\frac{3}{4}$ cup + 2 tablespoons water

$\frac{1}{4}$ cup olive oil

Steps for kneaded bread

Mix, knead, oil bowl

1st rise

Punch down, shape, 2nd rise

Prepare topping

Add topping and egg wash

Bake at 500° for 20–25
minutes

Steps for bread machines

Put in bread machine to mix,
knead, and rise

Remove dough after 1st rise to
finish by hand

Peppery Cilantro Focaccia

Topping
Crushed chile pepper to taste
$\frac{2}{3}$ cup fresh cilantro, chopped
small and packed

Dry ingredients
3 cups bread flour
2 $\frac{1}{4}$ teaspoons yeast
(same amount for bread
machines)
1 $\frac{1}{2}$ teaspoons salt
2 tablespoons crushed chile
pepper

Wet ingredients for kneaded bread
$\frac{3}{4}$ cup water
$\frac{1}{4}$ cup olive oil

Wet ingredients for bread machines
$\frac{3}{4}$ cup + 2 tablespoons water
$\frac{1}{4}$ cup olive oil

Steps for kneaded bread
Mix, knead, oil bowl
1st rise
Punch down, shape, 2nd rise
Prepare topping
Add topping and egg wash
Bake at 500° for 20–25
minutes

Steps for bread machines
Put in bread machine to mix,
knead, and rise
Remove dough after 1st rise to
finish by hand

Taco Salad Focaccia

Topping
2 cups hamburger
1 envelope taco seasoning
2 cups each lettuce and tomato, diced small
2 cups mild cheddar cheese,
  shredded
Cook and drain hamburger.
  Combine with taco seasoning,
  spread on top of focaccia
  dough, and bake. After baking, top with lettuce, tomato,
  and cheese.

Dry ingredients
3 cups bread flour
2¼ teaspoons yeast
  (same amount for bread
  machines)
1½ teaspoons salt

Wet ingredients for kneaded bread
¾ cup water
¼ cup olive oil

Wet ingredients for bread machines
¾ cup + 2 tablespoons water
¼ cup olive oil

Steps for kneaded bread
Mix, knead, oil bowl
1st rise
Punch down, shape, 2nd rise
Add hamburger topping and
  egg wash
Bake at 500° for 20–25
  minutes
Add salad topping

Steps for bread machines
Put in bread machine to mix,
  knead, and rise
Remove dough after 1st rise to
  finish by hand

FOCACCIA TOPPING VARIATIONS

Try some additional variations using just the basic focaccia dough plus any one of the following toppings. Unless directed otherwise, add the topping before baking.

Type of focaccia	Topping
Sage and Onion	2 cups red onion, thinly sliced ¼ cup fresh sage, chopped small
Red Onion and Fresh Rosemary	2 cups red onion, diced 4 tablespoons fresh rosemary, chopped
Marinated Artichoke Hearts with Onion	2 cups marinated artichoke hearts, thinly sliced and drained 1 cup red onion, diced small
Green Olives and Onions	1 cup green olives (salad) with pimentos 1 cup red onion both chopped small
Red, Yellow, and Green Bell Pepper with Fresh Oregano and Garlic	3 tablespoons fresh garlic, minced 1 cup each, yellow, red, and green bell pepper, diced 4 tablespoons fresh oregano, chopped small
Eggplant and Plum Tomatoes with Fresh Herbs	3 cups eggplant, diced small 3 cups plum tomatoes, sliced and drained on paper towels ¼ cup each fresh cilantro, basil, and oregano, chopped small and packed
Asparagus and Garlic	2½ cups tender asparagus tips 2 tablespoons garlic, minced ¼ cup fresh basil, chopped small and packed 1½ tablespoons butter Saute all ingredients in butter and drain.
Avocado Feta Salad	Bake focaccia with olive oil and let it cool. Top with: 2 cups alfalfa sprouts 1 cup each avocado and tomato, diced small 2 cups feta cheese, crumbled (or your choice).

Type of focaccia	Topping
Romano Cheese and Tomato	3 tablespoons garlic, minced 2 cups Romano cheese, shredded 2 large tomatoes, sliced medium thin (lay the slices on paper towels to absorb extra moisture)
Mushrooms and Cheese	2 cups provolone cheese, shredded 2 cups fresh Portabello mushrooms, thinly sliced
Broccoli and Cheese	3 cups fresh broccoli, chopped very small, blanched and drained 2½ cups American cheese, shredded Salt and pepper to taste
Pesto Mozzarella	2 cups pesto sauce 1 egg, beaten 1 cup mozzarella cheese, shredded Mix all and spread evenly on focaccia.
Tomato, Cheese, and Garlic	1 egg 1 cup tomato sauce 2 cups mozzarella cheese 1 tablespoon garlic, minced ¼ cup each fresh basil, oregano, cilantro, and parsley, chopped small and packed Beat egg into tomato sauce and mix in other ingredients.
Sausage and Savory	2 cups ground sausage (your choice), cooked and drained 4 tablespoons fresh savory, chopped small
Italian Sausage and Onion	2 cups Italian sausage, fried and drained 2 cups red onion, diced
Leeks and Pepperoni	2 cups pepperoni, diced small 1⅔ cups leeks, thinly sliced Saute together and drain.
Red Onion and Bacon	2 cups bacon, diced 1 cup red onion, diced small. Saute together and drain.

Type of focaccia	Topping
Smoked Ham and Smoked Cheese	2½ cups smoked cheese (your choice), shredded 2 cups smoked ham, diced small
Lemon Pepper Chicken with Cheese	3 large chicken breasts, fried in cooking spray, drained, and diced small lemon pepper, to taste 2 cups Monterey Jack cheese, shredded Coat chicken well with lemon pepper and mix with cheese. Sprinkle more lemon pepper around outside edges of crust.
Clams and Garlic	3 6-ounce cans chopped clams, drained, or equal amount of fresh clams 4 tablespoons garlic, minced 3 tablespoons fresh parsley, chopped small (no stems) 2 tablespoons butter Saute clams and garlic in butter and drain. Mix with parsley.
Shrimp	3 cups small shrimp, shelled and deveined 1 tablespoon garlic, minced 1 cup red onion, diced small 2 tablespoons butter Saute all ingredients in butter, drain, and spread evenly.
Smoked Salmon with Cream Cheese and Onion	1 8-ounce package of cream cheese 1 egg, beaten 2 cups smoked salmon (or your choice of fish) 1 cup red onion, diced small Cream the cheese with egg and spread evenly over the focaccia dough. Crumble salmon over the cheese mixture and top with onion.

STEPS FOR MAKING PIZZA

Use Basic Focaccia Recipe, page 223

Mix, knead, oil bowl, 1st rise as for focaccia

Punch down, shape, 2nd rise: Punch down to deflate. Divide the dough in half or leave whole for a large pizza. Roll out with a rolling pin or shape with the palms of your hands into a round about 14 inches in diameter and ¼ inch thick. Place on a well-sprayed cookie sheet or pizza pan. Pinch up edges of dough to form a lip around the pizza pie. Let rise 20–30 minutes. Preheat oven to 400°.

Add topping and bake: Spread topping evenly, leaving about ½ inch space all around the lip. Bake until the crust browns, about 12 minutes.

Basic topping
1–1½ cups your favorite pizza sauce
2–3 cups mozzarella cheese, shredded

Topping ideas
2–3 cups of any of the following (or your favorite combination):
- Meats: pepperoni, mild or hot cooked sausage (casings removed), seasoned hamburger, thinly sliced Canadian bacon or prosciutto, anchovies, smoked clams or oysters
- Vegetables, thinly sliced: mushrooms (raw or canned), onion, bell peppers—green, red, or yellow, black olives, marinated artichokes
- See Focaccia Topping Variations (pp. 234–236) for other ideas.

TRADITIONAL YEASTED FLATBREADS

Traditional flatbreads especially in India, the Near East, and northern Europe, are often made in individual serving sizes—rounds and other shapes. Some, like pitas, are "pocket" breads that can be stuffed with sandwich fillings. You can use white or whole grain flour for these breads.

Flatbread dough can be mixed and kneaded in your bread machine. Just remove after the first kneading, unless otherwise indicated.

Some flatbreads are made with sourdough starter. See the recipes for Ksra, a traditional Moroccan flatbread (p. 183), and Ciabatta, an Italian flatbread (p. 184).

Flatbreads are best served warm—fresh out of the oven.

Sopaipillas

I have adapted this Navajo fry bread for the oven. For frying, see instructions below the main recipe.

Dry Ingredients
3 cups bread flour
1 tablespoon yeast
(2¼ teaspoons for bread machines)
1 teaspoon salt
2 tablespoons sugar

Wet ingredients for kneaded bread
¾ cup milk
1 egg, beaten
1 tablespoon butter, melted

Wet ingredients for bread machines
¾ cup + 2 tablespoons milk
1 egg, beaten
1 tablespoon butter, melted

Steps for kneaded bread
Mix, knead until just smooth, place in oiled bowl. Cover and refrigerate for 2 hours. Spray a large baking sheet with cooking spray, divide dough into halves, and roll out into a round ¼ inch thick. Place one half on top of the other and roll together lightly, just enough to join—don't mash together completely. Cut into triangles from the center like pie wedges, and no larger than 3 inches at the widest part. Place on cookie sheet 1 inch apart. Bake at 475° for 8–10 minutes.

Steps for bread machines
Put in bread machine to mix and knead
Remove from machine to finish by hand

To fry sopaipillas: In a deep pan, heat 4–6 inches of oil. Test the oil by dropping a bit of dough into it; if the dough starts to fry, it is ready. Drop triangles of dough into the oil one piece at a time. Let each fry until it floats to the top. Turn it over, let it brown on the other side, remove, and drain.

Whole Wheat Pita

Dry ingredients
1 cup whole wheat flour (stone
   ground is especially good)
1 cup unbleached bread flour
2¼ teaspoons yeast
   (same amount for bread
   machines)
½ teaspoon salt

Wet ingredients for
kneaded bread
1 cup water
2 tablespoons olive oil

Wet ingredients for
bread machines
1 cup + 2 tablespoons water
2 tablespoon olive oil

Steps for kneaded bread:
Mix, knead, oil bowl. 1st rise
   (1 hour). Punch down, divide
   into 6 equal pieces. Shape
   into round balls, cover, and
   let rest 15 minutes. Roll out
6-inch rounds on a floured
surface. Preheat oven to
500°. Place a heavy baking
tray in the bottom of the
oven and preheat for 5 minutes. Remove the hot pan,
spray quickly with cooking
spray, and place as many circles on the tray as space
allows. Bake each batch for
10 minutes. (The pita should
puff up during baking and
deflate when removed from
the oven.) Serve fresh out of
the oven. To store pitas, let
cool thoroughly and place in
a plastic zip-lock bag.

Steps for bread machines
Put in bread machine to mix,
   knead, and rise
Remove from machine after
   1st rise to finish by hand

Naan

This delicious East Indian flatbread is puffy and light
and it cooks very quickly.

Dry ingredients

3¾ cups bread flour

2 teaspoons yeast

½ teaspoons salt

2 teaspoons sugar

1 teaspoon baking powder

Wet ingredients

⅔ cup milk

⅔ cup plain yogurt, lightly
   whipped

2 tablespoons olive oil

1 egg, beaten

Steps for kneaded bread

Mix, knead, oil bowl

1st rise

Punch down, 2nd rise

Preheat oven to 500°, and turn on the broiler. Place a heavy baking tray in the bottom of the oven. Knead dough 10 times and divide into 6 balls. Roll out in the traditional teardrop shape (an oval about 10 inches long, 5 inches wide). Remove the hot pan, spray quickly with cooking spray, and slap the dough on the pan. Return to the oven for 3 minutes. The dough should puff up. Place the pan under the broiler for another 30 seconds, or until the naan is golden brown. Reheat the pan briefly if more dough is to be baked.

Finnish Flatbread

This traditional rye flatbread is slightly sweet and good with any meal.

Dry ingredients
1½ cups bread flour
1½ cups rye flour
1 tablespoon yeast
(2¼ teaspoons for bread
machines)
1½ teaspoons salt
3 tablespoons brown sugar
(packed on the spoon)

**Wet ingredients for
kneaded bread**
¾ cup water
4 tablespoons butter, melted

**Wet ingredients for
bread machines**
¾–1 cup water
4 tablespoons butter, melted

Steps for kneaded bread
Mix (dough will be slightly tacky
but not sticky), knead. Spray
a baking pan with cooking
spray and sprinkle with ¼
cup cornmeal. Flatten the
dough with your fingers into
a 6-inch round. Place it on a
baking sheet and flatten to 9
inches in diameter. Spray
dough lightly with cooking
spray and cover loosely with
plastic wrap. 2nd rise (1½ to
2 hours). Bake at 425° for
15–20 minutes.

Steps for bread machines
Put in bread machine to mix
and knead
Remove from machine to finish
by hand

XII
Rolls, Buns, and Bialys

Most recipes in this book can be used to make any roll or bun of your choice. Even batter breads make a nice roll—just fill muffin tins halfway with the batter and bake. If you are a novice at making rolls, though, I suggest you start with the Basic Roll Recipe on the following page and experiment with other bread recipes once you're familiar with the process of shaping and baking these small breads. Rolls or buns can be filled with any flavorful addition you choose, provided it is not runny—a filling that is too liquid will make the rolls soggy.

Baking times will vary with the size of the rolls or buns. If you decide you want bite-sized rolls, set your timer for 5–8 minutes and bake until they are golden brown. Set the timer for another few minutes if the rolls haven't browned enough. For medium rolls, set your timer for 10 minutes or more. Hamburger or hotdog buns will take a little longer. You'll soon get a feel for baking times for the shapes you create.

Any kneaded bread dough can be refrigerated for a softer, more bunlike dough. Refrigeration slows the growth of yeast, giving the dough a chance to rest. After kneading, dough can become resistant; refrigerating makes it more responsive. Refrigerating the dough for 2 hours before the final rise will improve it—and give you a break to clean up any breadmaking mess in your kitchen.

Prepare a cookie sheet or muffin tin with cooking spray. Final rising time will vary because of the difference in shapes.

Basic Roll Recipe with Non-Fat Option

Makes 6–8 medium-sized rolls. Follow detailed steps in Chapter II pages 15–16, for mixing, kneading, and 1st rise.

Dry ingredients
3 cups bread flour
1 tablespoon yeast
(2¼ teaspoons for bread
machines)
1 teaspoon salt
1 tablespoon sugar

**Wet ingredients for
batter rolls**
1¾ cups water
1 tablespoon oil (optional)

**Wet ingredients for
kneaded rolls**
1 cup water
1 tablespoon oil (optional)

**Wet ingredients for
bread machines**
1⅛–1¼ cups water
1 tablespoon oil (optional)

Steps for kneaded rolls
Mix, knead, oil bowl
1st rise—up to an hour,
until doubled
Punch down, divide dough, follow directions for shaping
Refrigerate for 2 hours
(optional)
2nd rise (on sprayed pan)—
30–45 minutes, until doubled
Follow directions in recipes
for crust
Bake at 350° for 5–20 minutes
(depending on size)
Test for doneness and cool

Steps for bread machines
Put in bread machine to mix,
knead, and rise
Remove dough after 1st rise to
finish by hand

SHAPING AND BAKING ROLLS AND BUNS

Crescent Rolls

After 1st rise, roll dough into a rectangle ¼-inch thick, cut into triangles, and brush with melted butter. Roll up, starting with the wide end. 2nd rise. Bake at 350⁰ for 20 minutes.

Crust: soft
Brush rolls with milk *before* baking, or brush rolls with melted butter *after* baking.

Braided Rolls

After 1st rise, form dough into 3 long ropes and braid. Cut into desired lengths for rolls and pinch the ends. 2nd rise. Bake at 350⁰ for 10–15 minutes.

Crust: topping of sesame or poppy seeds
Prepare egg wash: Mix 1 beaten egg with 1 tablespoon milk or water. Before baking, brush with egg wash, sprinkle with topping, and brush with egg wash again, using a patting motion.

Corkscrews

After 1st rise, roll dough out to ½ inch thick. Cut into ½ inch strips 6–8 inches long. Wrap each strip around a greased wooden clothespin (the kind no metal) to form a spiral. The coils should touch each other. Pinch ends to last coil to close. 2nd rise. Bake at 375⁰ for 10–15 minutes. Remove the clothespins.

Crust: soft
Brush rolls with melted butter after baking.

Cloverleaf Rolls

After 1st rise, shape dough into balls about 1 inch in diameter. Place three balls in each greased muffin tin. 2nd rise. Bake at 350⁰ for 15–20 minutes.

Crust: soft
Brush rolls with milk *before* baking, or brush loaf with melted butter *after* baking.

Parkerhouse Rolls

After 1st rise, roll dough out to ½ inch thick. Using a 3 inch cookie cutter or glass, cut circles in the dough. Roll just the centers of the circles to shape circles into ovals. Brush the centers with butter, and fold the dough in half. Pinch the sides shut. 2nd rise. Bake at 400° for 15–20 minutes.

Crust: soft
Brush rolls with melted butter after baking.

Twist Rolls

After 1st rise, roll dough out into a rectangle ½ inch thick. Cut into ½ inch strips. Pinching ends together, twist 2 strips together, and cut into desired lengths. Pinch ends together to seal. 2nd rise. Bake at 400° for 10–15 minutes.

Crust: your choice
(See pp. 22–23)

Leaf Buds

After 1st rise, shape dough into 2 inch balls. Place 2 balls in each greased muffin tin. 2nd rise. Bake at 375° for 20 minutes.

Crust: soft
Brush rolls with milk *before* baking, or brush rolls with melted butter *after* baking.

Bowknots

After 1st rise, roll dough into long ropes ½ inch thick and cut into 6 inch strips. Tie a lose knot and pinch the ends underneath to close. 2nd rise. Bake at 375° for 20 minutes.

Crust: topping of seeds (your choice)
Prepare egg wash: Mix 1 beaten egg with 1 tablespoon milk or water. Before baking, brush with egg wash, sprinkle with topping, and brush with egg wash again, using a patting motion.

Fantails

After 1st rise, roll dough into a rectangle 10 to 12 inches long and ½ inch thick. Divide into even strips no more than 1½–2 inches wide, and pile the strips on top of one another. Cut into 2–3 inch lengths, and pinch one end shut. Brush each layer with melted butter and place, pinched end down, in a greased muffin tin. 2nd rise. Bake at 400° for 20 minutes.

Crust: soft
Brush rolls with melted butter after baking.

Round Rolls

After 1st rise, shape dough into desired sized balls and place on a greased cookie sheet. 2nd rise. Bake at 400° for 20–25 minutes.

Crust: your choice
(See pp. 22–23)

Pinwheels

After 1st rise, roll dough out into a rectangle 10–12 inches long and ½ inch thick. Cut into strips 2 inches wide and the length of the rectangle. Roll each strip into a spiral (like a cinnamon roll). Pinch the end to seal and place in a greased muffin tin. Bake at 400° for 20 minutes.

Crust: soft
Brush rolls with melted butter after baking.

Circle Twist Rolls

After 1st rise, roll dough out to ½ inch thick. Cut into 1 inch strips 4½ inches long. Twist each strip into a circle and pinch the ends to seal. 2nd rise. Bake at 375° for 15–20 minutes.

Crust: your choice
(See pp. 22–23)

Hard Rolls

After 1st rise, shape into 8 to 10 balls, depending on the size you want. They will be somewhat smaller than a hamburger bun. Flatten out slightly. 2nd rise. Bake at 400° for 10–15 minutes or until golden brown.

Crust: crisp
Using a spray bottle, spray the rolls 4 times with cold water during baking.

Hamburger Buns

After 1st rise, divide into 6 to 8 pieces, depending on the size you need. Shape into balls and flatten slightly. 2nd rise (until doubled in size). Bake at 350° for 15–20 minutes.

Crust: soft
Brush rolls with milk *before* baking, or brush rolls with melted butter *after* baking.

Hot Dog Buns

After 1st rise, shape dough into 6 to 8 balls, depending on the size you need. Roll into an oblong shape and flatten out slightly. 2nd rise (until doubled in size). Bake at 350° for 15–20 minutes.

Crust: soft
Brush rolls with milk *before* baking, or brush rolls with melted butter *after* baking.

Pretzels

After 1st rise, shape dough into long ropes. Cut to desired length and shape into pretzels. 2nd rise. Bake at 400° for 15–20 minutes.

Crust: topping of seeds (your choice)
Prepare egg wash: Mix 1 beaten egg with 1 tablespoon milk or water. Before baking, brush with egg wash, sprinkle with topping, and brush with egg wash again, using a patting motion.

Savory Swirls

After 1st rise, roll dough out to a rectangle about 16 x 14 inches and $\frac{1}{4}$ inch thick. For savory swirls, use cooked, drained, ground meat (such as sausage), or another meat (ham, chicken), vegetable, diced very small, or shredded cheese. Spread evenly over the dough, leaving 1 inch on one of the longer sides empty, so that you can pinch the end shut after the dough is rolled up. Starting with the other long side, roll up like a jelly roll and pinch the seam closed. Using a sharp bread knife, cut the roll into slices 1–2 inches thick. Place slices, flat side down, on a cookie sheet that has been well prepared with cooking spray. 2nd rise. Bake at 400° for 15–20 minutes or until golden brown.

Crust: soft
Brush rolls with melted butter after baking.

Stuffed Rolls

After 1st rise, shape dough into 1 inch balls. Roll out into circles $\frac{1}{2}$ inch thick. Place 1 teaspoon of finely diced meat, cheese, or vegetable (well drained) on half of the circles. (The filling should be dry; otherwise you will end up with a soggy roll.) Cover each with another circle and pinch the edges together. 2nd rise. Bake at 350° for 15–20 minutes.

Crust: your choice
(See pp. 22–23)

English Muffins

Topping
Yellow cornmeal (in a shallow bowl) to coat the muffins

Dry ingredients
3 cups bread flour
1 tablespoon yeast
1 teaspoon salt
1 tablespoon sugar

Wet ingredients
1 cup milk
2 tablespoons olive oil

Steps
Mix, knead, oil bowl
1st rise
Punch down (do not knead), 2nd rise (10 minutes). Roll out to ¼ inch thick. Using a 4 inch cookie cutter or glass, cut out circles. Dip both sides in cornmeal to coat. Cover. 3rd rise (30 minutes).

Pan fry: In a large, ungreased frying pan, cook muffins for about 20–25 minutes over medium to low heat, turning frequently. If you do not have room for all the muffins, use two pans or cover the remaining muffins and refrigerate until ready to cook.

Variation: You can make Whole Wheat English Muffins by omitting 1 cup of white flour and adding 1 cup of whole wheat flour. Experiment with other flours.

Edith's Buns

This recipe also makes wonderful hamburger or hotdog buns.

Dry ingredients
3 cups bread flour
1 tablespoon yeast
(2¼ teaspoons for bread
machines)
1½ teaspoons salt
1½ teaspoons sugar

**Wet ingredients for
kneaded buns**
1 cup milk
2 tablespoons olive oil

**Wet ingredients for
bread machines**
¾ cup + 2 tablespoons water
2 tablespoons olive oil

Steps for kneaded buns
Mix, knead, oil bowl
1st rise (until tripled in size)
Punch down, 2nd rise. Shape
into 8 to 10 round rolls,
depending on the size you
want
3rd rise (30 minutes)
Crust: sesame seed topping, or
your choice
Bake at 350° for 20–25
minutes, depending on size
Cool and serve

Steps for bread machines
Put in bread machine to mix,
knead, and rise
Remove dough after 1st rise to
finish by hand

Crust: topping of sesame seeds (or your choice)
Prepare egg wash: Mix 1 beaten egg with
1 tablespoon milk or water. Before baking, brush
with egg wash, sprinkle with topping, and brush
with egg wash again, using a patting motion.

Good-for-You One-Hour-Rise Rolls

Topping
Sesame seeds

Dry ingredients
1½ cups bread flour
1 cup oat flour
¼ cup wheat germ
¼ cup soy flour
1 tablespoon yeast
  (2¼ teaspoons for bread
  machines)
1½ teaspoons salt

**Wet ingredients for
kneaded rolls**
¾ cup milk
¼ cup honey
1½ tablespoons olive oil

**Wet ingredients for
bread machines**
¾ cup + 2 tablespoons milk
¼ cup honey
1½ tablespoons olive oil

Steps for kneaded rolls
Mix, knead
Divide into 8 to 10 pieces.
  Shape (your choice)
1st rise (1 hour)
Add topping
Bake at 375° for 15–20
  minutes, depending on size.
  Cool and serve

Steps for bread machines
Put in bread machine to mix,
  knead, and rise
Remove dough after 1st rise to
  finish by hand

Crust: topping of sesame seeds
Prepare egg wash: Mix 1 beaten egg with
1 tablespoon milk or water. Before baking,
brush with egg wash, sprinkle with topping,
and brush with egg wash again, using a
patting motion.

Brown-and-Serve Dinner Rolls

Pre-bake, then freeze or store in refrigerator

Dry ingredients

3 cups bread flour
1 tablespoon yeast
  (2¼ teaspoons for bread
  machines)
1½ teaspoons salt
1½ teaspoons sugar

**Wet ingredients for
kneaded rolls**
1 cup milk

**Wet ingredients for
bread machines**
1 cup + 2 tablespoons milk

Steps for kneaded rolls

Mix, knead, oil bowl
1st rise
Punch down, 2nd rise. Divide
  into 8. Shape into round rolls
  (or shape of your choice).
Bake at 400° for 10 minutes.

Crust: soft
Brush loaf with milk *before*
  baking.
  Or
Brush loaf with melted but-
  ter *after* baking.

Steps for bread machines

Put in bread machine to mix,
  knead, and rise
Remove dough after 1st rise to
  finish by hand
Store in a plastic bag and
  refrigerate for up to a week.
  Or flash-freeze: Place the
  rolls on a well-sprayed cookie
  sheet 1 inch apart. Spray the
  rolls well with cooking spray
  (to keep them from drying
  out), cover with plastic wrap.
  Place in the freezer and leave
  until hard. Remove from the
  cookie sheet and store in a
  plastic bag.
Remove rolls as needed. Cover
  with plastic wrap that has
  been sprayed with cooking
  spray, and let rise in a warm
  place for 2–4 hours, or until
  doubled in size. Bake at 400°
  for 15 minutes (or until
  golden brown), and cool.

Bialys

A specialty of Bialystok, Poland, these savory rolls are especially good with cream cheese or used as a hamburger bun. Recipe makes about 6 bialys.

Dry ingredients

2 cups bread flour
1 cup light rye flour
1 tablespoon yeast
1½ teaspoons salt
2 teaspoons sugar
½ teaspoon freshly ground black or regular pepper (optional)

Topping

¼ cup red onion, thinly sliced and diced small
1 tablespoon butter
1 tablespoon poppy seeds
Pinch of salt
Saute onion in butter, and drain. Stir in poppy seeds and salt.

Wet ingredients

1 cup water

Steps

Mix, knead, oil bowl
1st rise (30 minutes), punch down. Press flat with your fingers to get rid of bubbles. Shape into six 3½ inch balls (handle the dough lightly to avoid kneading). Using your fingers, press out to about 1 inch thick. Cover. 2nd rise (30 minutes). Spray the bottom of a glass 1–2 inches in diameter. Make an indentation in the middle of the dough with the glass, and sprinkle with the topping mixture. Repeat for all the rolls. Dust the whole roll lightly with flour. Cover.
3rd rise (15 minutes)
Crust: very chewy
Bake at 450° degrees for 15 minutes and cool

Crust: very chewy

Prepare egg wash: Mix 1 beaten egg with 1 tablespoon milk or water. Before baking, brush the edges outside the indentation with egg wash. Then steam: Place a pan on the floor of the oven. Preheat oven to full heat. Toss 6 to 8 ice cubes into the pan, place the bialys in right away, and close the door quickly.

Croissants

Dry ingredients
3½ cups unbleached bread
 flour
1 tablespoon yeast
 (2¼ teaspoons for bread
 machines)
½ teaspoon salt
1 tablespoon sugar
1 cup butter, very cold, cut into
 small squares

Wet ingredients for kneaded rolls and bread machines
1 cup milk
¼ cup water
2 eggs, beaten

Steps for kneaded rolls
Mix dry ingredients together
 with a pastry blender, until the
 flour takes on the consistency
 of large peas. Add wet ingredients, and mix until a dough
 is formed. Refrigerate for 3
 hours. Knead lightly. Divide
 into thirds, and roll each piece
of dough into a circle about
 14 inches in diameter. Cut
 each circle into 12 wedges
 (like a pie). Roll each wedge,
 starting with the widest end.
 Place rolls point down on a
 baking sheet that has been
 sprayed with cooking spray.
 Cover and let rise 30–45 minutes, or until doubled.
Crust: shiny
Bake at 375° degrees for 20
 minutes, or until golden
 brown, serve.

Steps for bread machines
Put in bread machine to mix,
 knead, and rise
Remove dough after 1st rise to
 finish by hand

Variations: See Sweet
Croissants (p. 262).

Crust: shiny
Mix 1 beaten egg with 1 tablespoon milk
or water. Before baking, brush loaf with
egg wash.

Onion Pockets

Makes about 6 pockets.

Dry ingredients
3 cups bread flour
1 tablespoon yeast
   (2 ¼ teaspoons for bread
   machines)
1 teaspoon salt

Filling
1 ½ cups red onion, diced small
1 tablespoon butter
1 tablespoon each poppy and
   sesame seeds
3 tablespoons fresh basil,
   minced small
Saute onion in butter and
   drain. Mix in other
   ingredients.

Wet ingredients for
kneaded pockets
1 cup water

Wet ingredients for
bread machines
1 cup + 2 tablespoons water

Steps for kneaded pockets
Mix, knead, oil bowl
1st rise
Punch down, 2nd rise. Shape
   8–10 round balls and roll out
   to circles ¼ inch thick. Place
   a tablespoon of filling in the
   center of each, and seal by
   pinching the edges. Cover.
3rd rise (20 minutes)
Bake at 375^0 for 25–30
   minutes and cool

Steps for bread machines
Put in bread machine to mix,
   knead, and rise
Remove dough after 1st rise to
   finish by hand

XIII
Sweet Rolls and Dessert Breads

SWEET ROLLS AND BUNS

A simple sweet dough can be the basis for many different sweet rolls in a variety of shapes and flavors. The dough is easy to make and easy to handle. It can be baked immediately or refrigerated if you want a softer dough (more like a bun). The dough is very good either way. If you want to use whole wheat or other whole grain flour, omit 1 cup of white bread flour and add 1 cup of the flour of choice. Just remember to have all the recommended dry ingredients and recommended wet ingredients at the proper temperature.

Always spray your cooking surface with cooking spray. The baking time varies depending on the size of the rolls you make. Start off by setting your timer at 10 minutes (5 minutes if you are making bite-size rolls) and keep checking. According to size, you should get 6–8 rolls from the basic recipe below.

Refrigerated overnight, this dough is excellent for cinnamon buns. In the morning, shape into buns, let rise, and bake. They make a good breakfast treat for a weekend.

The directions in Chapter XII (pp. 245-249) can be used for shaping sweet rolls and buns.

Basic Sweet Dough

Dry ingredients
3 cups bread flour
1 tablespoon yeast
  (2 ¼ teaspoons for bread
  machines)
1 teaspoon salt
½ cup brown sugar

Wet ingredients for kneaded rolls
½ cup milk
½ cup melted butter
2 eggs, beaten

Wet ingredients for bread machines
½ cup + 2 tablespoons milk
½ cup melted butter
2 eggs, beaten

Steps for kneaded rolls
Mix, knead, oil bowl
1st rise
Punch down, 2nd rise
Shape (your choice,
  pp. 20–21), 3rd rise
Bake at 400⁰ for 20–25
  minutes, or until golden brown
Top with glaze (optional, pp.
  259–260)

Steps for kneaded rolls, refrigerated dough
Mix, knead, oil bowl
Cover the dough with plastic
  wrap, refrigerate overnight.
Remove and let rise 1–2 hours.
  Punch down and knead a few
  times.
Shape (your choice), let rise
  30–45 minutes
Bake at 400⁰ for 20–25 min-
  utes or until golden brown
Top with glaze (optional, pp.
  259–60))

Steps for bread machines
Use bread machine through
  2nd rise cycle
Remove from machine to punch
  down and finish by hand

GLAZES

The glaze recipes in this book are some of the simplest in the world—and delicious. The basic recipe calls for 1 cup of confectioner's sugar (powdered sugar), a hot liquid, and often a dry ingredient or an extract for flavor. A few drops of melted butter can be added for flavor and texture. The amount of liquid you use depends upon whether you want a glaze that you can pour over the roll or one that is thick enough to apply with a knife. More liquid will be required if you are adding an extra dry ingredient, such as cocoa powder.

The liquid should be added a tablespoon at a time to keep the glaze from becoming too runny. When using a flavored extract, add it sparingly and mix it with the liquid before adding sugar.

Basic Glaze Recipe

1 cup confectioner's sugar (powdered sugar)
Other dry ingredient (see table, next page)
2–3 tablespoons hot liquid
1–2 drops flavored extract per tablespoon of liquid

A few drops melted butter (optional)
Mix hot liquid with flavored extract (if called for). Add to sugar 1 tablespoon at a time, mixing thoroughly.

Glaze Variations

(Made with 1 cup powdered sugar)

Name of glaze	Dry ingredients	Liquid (2–3 tablespoons)
Chocolate	3 heaping tablespoons cocoa powder	hot water + a drop of vanilla extract (optional)
Orange	2 tablespoons fresh orange zest	hot orange juice
Lemon	2 tablespoons fresh lemon zest	hot lemon juice
Honey		hot honey
Coffee		extra strong coffee
Maple		hot water + a few drops of maple flavoring
Eggnog		hot eggnog
Liqueur, Rum, or Brandy		Irish cream or your choice
Peppermint	crushed peppermint candy (enough to sprinkle thinly on each bun)	hot water + a few drops of peppermint extract
Strawberry or Blueberry	3 tablespoons defrosted and mashed frozen berries in heavy syrup (drained and reserved)	the heavy syrup, heated
Almond, Vanilla, Cinnamon, Rum, etc.		hot water + a few drops of extract
Cinnamon	1 teaspoon cinnamon-sugar	

Cinnamon Rolls

Made right away or refrigerated overnight, cinnamon rolls can be made with the recipe for either Basic Sweet Dough (p. 258) or Edith's Buns (p. 250). Use larger amounts of the extra ingredients if you like a sweeter or richer roll.

Extra ingredients
½–¾ cup melted butter
½–¾ cup cinnamon-sugar
 (1 heaping tablespoon
 cinnamon to 1 cup sugar)

½–¾ cup walnuts or pecans,
 finely chopped (optional)

After first rise, roll dough out to a rectangle about 16 x14 inches and ¼ inch thick. Spread melted butter evenly over the dough, leaving 1 inch on one long side empty. Cover the butter evenly with cinnamon-sugar and nuts, and roll up the dough like a jelly roll, starting with the other long side. Pinch the seam closed. Using a sharp bread knife, cut the roll into slices 1–2 inches thick, with a gentle sawing motion. Place slices, flat side down, on a cookie sheet that has been well prepared with cooking spray. 2nd rise. Bake at 400° for 15–20 minutes or until golden brown. Serve warm from the oven.

Sweet Croissants

Sweet fillings for croissants must be thinly spread and must not become runny when baked, or they will spoil the roll. For these treats, follow the recipe on page 255 for 12 croissants.

Jam Croissants

You can flavor them with raspberry, blueberry, apricot, black currant, or other favorite preserves, or with marmalade—or make a dozen assorted croissants.

Spread no more than 1 tablespoon of your favorite preserve on each wedge of dough, leaving an inch at the tip empty to seal the roll. Roll up, starting at the wide end, pinch to seal, and place, point down, on a sprayed baking sheet.

White Chocolate Croissants

White chocolate is delicious.

Sprinkle 2 tablespoons white mini-chocolate chips on each wedge of dough, leaving an inch empty at the tip to seal the roll. Roll up, starting at the wide end, pinch to seal, and place, point down, on a sprayed baking sheet.

Crust: shiny
Mix 1 beaten egg with 1 tablespoon milk or water. Before baking, brush loaf with egg wash.

Raised Doughnuts

The key to good doughnuts is oil temperature. You will need a good candy thermometer and a deep pot that will hold 2–4 quarts. The oil should be 4 inches deep. The large pot minimizes splattering and keeps the oil at a more even temperature.

Dry ingredients
3½ cups all purpose flour
1 tablespoon yeast
1 teaspoon salt
¼ cup sugar

Wet ingredients
1 cup milk
¼ cup butter, melted
2 eggs, beaten

Variations: Orange doughnuts: Omit ½ cup milk and replace it with ½ cup orange juice + 4 tablespoons orange zest.
Jellied doughnuts: After the 2nd rise, roll out to ½ inch thick and cut into 2½-inch circles using a glass or biscuit cutter. Place 1 teaspoon of your favorite jelly or preserves in the center. Seal the edges with egg wash (p. 22). Fold over and seal carefully. Fry in oil 1 minute on each side. Drain and add sugar, powdered sugar, or glaze.

Steps for doughnuts
Mix, knead, oil bowl
1st rise
Punch down, 2nd rise. Roll out to ½ inch thick and cut with a floured doughnut cutter.
Cover and let rise for 45 minutes. Heat oil to 360° and carefully drop 1–2 doughnuts at a time into the oil. Fry for 1 minute or until golden brown. With a slotted spoon, turn doughnuts over and fry an additional 1 minute or until golden brown. Remove and drain on a paper towel.
Coating: granulated sugar, powdered sugar, or glaze

Granulated sugar coating: Toss in sugar while doughnuts are still wet.
Powdered sugar coating: Toss in sugar after the doughnut has dried.
Glaze: See page 260 for glaze of your choice

DESSERT BREADS

These breads are often called dinner breads or tea breads. The dessert bread recipes in this chapter call for a 9 x 4 inch loaf pan. I offer a basic sweet bread recipe, which is a little richer than other types of breads. You can cut down on the amount of melted butter, but remember to adjust total liquid content to make sure the dough is moist enough. Since this is a treat rather than a "daily bread," the butter content may not be a problem.

When you get the hang of making this kind of bread, you can adapt other recipes—especially those for whole grain breads—for a dessert type treat—by substituting a portion of whole grain flour for the bread flour. (My recommendation is 2 cups bread flour to 1 cup whole grain.) You can also create your own variations using fruits, nuts, and other favorite additions.

Dessert breads can be molded into any shape you wish. If you are using a bread machine and wish to hand-shape the bread, remove the loaf from the machine after the 2nd rise to shape and bake it the old-fashioned way.

I recommend a simple glaze for each bread recipe, and a choice of other glazes are given on page 260. You may find, though, that the bread is sweet and tasty enough without a glaze.

Basic Sweet Bread Recipe

Dry ingredients

3 cups bread flour

1 tablespoon yeast
   (2¼ teaspoons for bread
   machines)

1 teaspoon salt

½ cup brown or white sugar

Wet ingredients for kneaded bread

½ cup milk

½ cup melted butter

1 egg, beaten

Wet ingredients for bread machines

½ cup + 2 tablespoons milk

½ cup melted butter

1 egg, beaten

Steps for kneaded bread

Mix, knead, oil bowl

1st rise

Punch down, 2nd rise

Shape into loaf (or shape of
   your choice), 3rd rise

Bake at 375⁰ for 40–45
   minutes

Test for doneness and cool

Steps for bread machines

Put in bread machine to mix,
   knead, and rise

Remove after 2nd rise to
   punch down and finish by
   hand

Lemon Poppy Bread

Dry ingredients

3 cups bread flour

1 tablespoon yeast
(2¼ teaspoons for bread
machines)

1 teaspoon salt

½ cup brown or white sugar

3½ tablespoons poppy seeds

4 tablespoons lemon zest

Wet ingredients for kneaded bread

½ cup lemon juice

½ cup melted butter

1 egg, beaten

1 teaspoon lemon extract

Wet ingredients for bread machines

¾ cup milk

½ cup melted butter

1 egg, beaten

Steps for kneaded bread

Mix, knead, oil bowl

1st rise

Punch down, 2nd rise

Shape into loaf (or shape of
your choice), 3rd rise

Bake at 375° for 40–45
minutes

Test for doneness and cool

Top with Lemon Glaze
(optional)

Steps for bread machines

Put in bread machine to mix,
knead, and rise

Remove after 2nd rise to
punch down and finish by
hand

Lemon glaze

Mix and apply while hot:

1 cup powdered sugar

2 tablespoons fresh lemon zest

2–3 tablespoons hot lemon juice

A few drops melted butter (optional)

Date Black Walnut Bread

Dry ingredients
3 cups bread flour
1 tablespoon yeast
  (2 ¼ teaspoons for bread
  machines)
1 teaspoon salt
½ cup brown or white sugar
1 cup black walnuts,
  chopped small
1 cup dried dates,
  chopped small
1 teaspoon ground cinnamon

Wet ingredients for kneaded bread
½ cup milk
½ cup melted butter
1 egg, beaten

Wet ingredients for bread machines
¾ cup milk
½ cup melted butter
1 egg, beaten

Steps for kneaded bread
Mix, knead, oil bowl
1st rise
Punch down, 2nd rise
Shape into loaf (or shape of
  your choice), 3rd rise
Bake at 375° for 40–45
  minutes
Test for doneness and cool
Top with: Honey Glaze
  (optional)

Steps for bread machines
Put in bread machine to mix,
  knead, and rise
Remove after 2nd rise to
  punch down and finish by
  hand

Honey Glaze
Mix and apply while hot:
1 cup powdered sugar
2–3 tablespoons hot honey
A few drops melted butter

Apple Spice Nut Bread

Dry ingredients
2 cups bread flour
1 cup whole wheat flour
1 tablespoon yeast
(2¼ teaspoons for bread
machines)
1 teaspoon salt
½ cup brown or white sugar
1 cup nuts (your choice),
chopped small
½ cup Granny Smith apples,
diced small
1 tablespoon allspice, or
to taste

**Wet ingredients for
kneaded bread**
½ cup milk
½ cup apple sauce
1 egg, beaten
1 tablespoon melted butter

**Wet ingredients for
bread machines**
¾ cup milk
½ cup applesauce
1 tablespoon melted butter
1 egg, beaten
1 tablespoon melted butter

Steps for kneaded bread
Mix, knead, oil bowl
1st rise
Punch down, 2nd rise
Shape into loaf (or shape of
your choice), 3rd rise
Bake at 375° for 40–45
minutes
Test for doneness and cool
Top with Orange Glaze
(optional)

Steps for bread machines
Put in bread machine to mix,
knead, and rise
Remove after 2nd rise to punch
down and finish by hand

Orange Glaze
Mix and apply while hot:
1 cup powdered sugar
2 tablespoons fresh orange zest
2–3 tablespoons hot orange juice
A few drops melted butter

Macadamia Nut Raisin Bread

Dry ingredients

3 cups bread flour

1 tablespoon yeast
  (2 ¼ teaspoons for bread
  machines)

1 teaspoon salt

½ cup brown or white sugar

1 cup raisins

½ cup macadamia nuts,
  chopped small

2 teaspoons cinnamon

**Wet ingredients for
kneaded bread**

½ cup milk

½ cup melted butter

1 egg, beaten

**Wet ingredients for
bread machines**

¾ cup milk

½ cup melted butter

1 egg, beaten

Steps for kneaded bread

Mix, knead, oil bowl

1st rise

Punch down, 2nd rise

Shape into loaf (or shape of
  your choice), 3rd rise

Bake at 375° for 40–45
  minutes

Test for doneness and cool

Top with Irish Cream Liqueur
  Glaze (optional)

Steps for bread machines

Put in bread machine to mix,
  knead, and rise

Remove after 2nd rise to punch
  down and finish by hand

Irish Cream Liqueur Glaze
Mix and apply while hot:
1 cup powdered sugar
2–3 tablespoons hot Irish Cream
A few drops melted butter (optional)

Cranberry Nut Bread

Dry ingredients
3 cups bread flour
1 tablespoon yeast
   (2 $\frac{1}{4}$ teaspoons for bread
   machines)
1 teaspoon salt
$\frac{1}{2}$ cup brown or white sugar
1 cup roasted brazil nuts,
   chopped small

Wet ingredients for kneaded bread
$\frac{1}{2}$ cup cranberry juice
$\frac{1}{2}$ cup melted butter
1 egg, beaten
1 cup canned whole (not jellied)
   cranberries

Wet ingredients for bread machines
$\frac{3}{4}$ cup cranberry juice
$\frac{1}{2}$ cup melted butter
1 egg, beaten
1 cup canned whole (not jellied)
   cranberries

Steps for kneaded bread
Mix, knead, oil bowl
1st rise
Punch down, 2nd rise
Shape into loaf (or shape of
   your choice), 3rd rise
Bake at 375^0 for 40–45
   minutes
Test for doneness and cool
Top with Orange Glaze
   (optional)

Steps for bread machines
Put in bread machine to mix,
   knead, and rise
Remove after 2nd rise to punch
   down and finish by hand

Orange Glaze
Mix and apply while hot:
1 cup powdered sugar
2 tablespoons fresh orange zest
2–3 tablespoons hot orange juice
A few drops melted butter

Orange Almond Bread

Dry ingredients
3 cups bread flour
1 tablespoon yeast
  (2 $\frac{1}{4}$ teaspoons for bread
  machines)
1 teaspoon salt
$\frac{1}{2}$ cup brown or white sugar
1 cup toasted slivered almonds

Wet ingredients for kneaded bread
$\frac{1}{2}$ cup orange juice
$\frac{1}{2}$ cup melted butter
1 egg, beaten

Wet ingredients for bread machines
$\frac{3}{4}$ cup orange juice
$\frac{1}{2}$ cup melted butter
1 egg, beaten

Steps for kneaded bread
Mix, knead, oil bowl
1st rise
Punch down, 2nd rise
Shape into loaf (or shape of
  your choice), 3rd rise
Bake at 375° for 40–45
  minutes
Test for doneness and cool
Top with Orange Glaze
  (optional)

Steps for bread machines
Put in bread machine to mix,
  knead, and rise
Remove after 2nd rise to punch
  down and finish by hand

Orange Glaze
Mix and apply while hot:
1 cup powdered sugar
2 tablespoons fresh orange zest
2–3 tablespoons hot orange juice
A few drops melted butter

Hazelnut and Golden Raisin Bread

Dry ingredients
3 cups bread flour

1 tablespoon yeast
(2¼ teaspoons for bread machines)

1 teaspoon salt

½ cup brown or white sugar

1 cup toasted hazelnuts, chopped small

1 cup golden raisins

Wet ingredients for kneaded bread
½ cup milk

½ cup melted butter

1 egg, beaten

Wet ingredients for bread machines
¾ cup milk

½ cup melted butter

1 egg, beaten

Steps for kneaded bread
Mix, knead, oil bowl

1st rise

Punch down, 2nd rise

Shape into loaf (or shape of your choice), 3rd rise

Bake at 375° for 40–45 minutes

Test for doneness and cool

Top with Maple Glaze (optional)

Steps for bread machines
Put in bread machine to mix, knead, and rise

Remove after 2nd rise to punch down and finish by hand

Maple Glaze
Mix and apply while hot:

1 cup powdered sugar

2–3 tablespoons hot water

A few drops maple flavoring

A few drops melted butter (optional)

Chocolate-Chocolate Bread

One of my favorites.

Dry ingredients

3 cups bread flour

1 tablespoon yeast
(2¼ teaspoons for bread machines)

1 teaspoon salt

½ cup brown or white sugar

6 heaping tablespoons unsweetened cocoa powder

1 cup chocolate chips

Wet ingredients for kneaded bread

½ cup milk

½ cup melted butter

1 egg, beaten

Wet ingredients for bread machines

¾ cup milk

½ cup melted butter

1 egg, beaten

Steps for kneaded bread

Mix, knead, oil bowl

1st rise

Punch down, 2nd rise

Shape into loaf (or shape of your choice), 3rd rise

Bake at 375° for 40–45 minutes

Test for doneness and cool

Top with Chocolate Glaze (optional)

Steps for bread machines

Put in bread machine to mix, knead, and rise

Remove after 2nd rise to punch down and finish by hand

Chocolate Glaze

Mix and apply while hot:

1 cup powdered sugar

3 heaping tablespoons unsweetened cocoa powder

2–4 tablespoons hot water

A few drops melted butter

Cherry Chocolate Bread

Dry ingredients
3 cups bread flour
1 tablespoon yeast
  (2¼ teaspoons for bread
  machines)
1 teaspoon salt
½ cup brown or white sugar
6 heaping tablespoons
  unsweetened cocoa powder
½ teaspoon ground cinnamon

**Wet ingredients for
kneaded bread**
2 cups cherry pie filling, with
  heavy syrup
melted butter, 1 tablespoon at
  a time as needed
1 egg, beaten

**Wet ingredients for
bread machines**
2¼ cups cherry pie filling, with
  heavy syrup
melted butter, 1 tablespoon at
  a time as needed
1 egg, beaten

Steps for kneaded bread
Mix, knead, oil bowl
1st rise
Punch down, 2nd rise
Shape into loaf (or shape of
  your choice), 3rd rise
Bake at 375° for 40–45
  minutes
Test for doneness and cool

Steps for bread machines
Put in bread machine to mix,
  knead, and rise
Remove after 2nd rise to punch
  down and finish by hand

Glaze: your choice
(pp.259–260)

Ginger and Pear Bread

Dry ingredients
3 cups bread flour
1 tablespoon yeast
  (2¼ teaspoons for bread
  machines)
1 teaspoon salt
½ cup brown or white sugar
2 cups fresh ripe pears, diced
  very small

**Wet ingredients for
kneaded bread**
½ cup milk
½ cup melted butter
1 egg, beaten
2 tablespoons fresh ginger,
  grated

**Wet ingredients for
bread machines**
¾ cup milk
½ cup melted butter
1 egg, beaten
2 tablespoons fresh ginger,
  grated

Steps for kneaded bread
Mix, knead, oil bowl
1st rise
Punch down, 2nd rise
Shape into loaf (or shape of
  your choice), 3rd rise
Bake at 375⁰ for 40–45
  minutes
Test for doneness and cool
Top with Vanilla Glaze
  (optional)

Steps for bread machines
Put in bread machine to mix,
  knead, and rise
Remove after 2nd rise to punch
  down and finish by hand

Vanilla Glaze
Mix and apply while hot:
1 cup powdered sugar
2–3 tablespoons hot water
A few drops vanilla extract
A few drops melted butter

Eggnog Bread

Dry ingredients
3 cups bread flour
1 tablespoon yeast
(2¼ teaspoons for bread
machines)
1 teaspoon salt
½ cup brown or white sugar

Wet ingredients for kneaded bread
1 cup eggnog
1 egg, beaten

Wet ingredients for bread machines
1 cup eggnog
¼ cup milk
1 egg, beaten

Steps for kneaded bread
Mix, knead, oil bowl
1st rise
Punch down, 2nd rise
Shape into loaf (or shape of
your choice), 3rd rise
Bake at 375° for 40–45
minutes
Test for doneness and cool
Top with Eggnog Glaze
(optional)

Steps for bread machines
Put in bread machine to mix,
knead, and rise
Remove after 2nd rise to punch
down and finish by hand

Eggnog Glaze
Mix and apply while hot:
1 cup powdered sugar
2–3 tablespoons hot eggnog
A few drops melted butter

SWEET FOCACCIA

Dough recipe, steps, and baking time are the same as for savory focaccia—the only difference is the topping. For sweet focaccia, brush on ¼–½ cup melted butter instead of olive oil. After putting on the final topping, dab with melted butter again. Baking time is the same.

Follow Detailed Steps for Making Focaccia (p. 222) and Basic Focaccia Recipe (p. 223).

Fruit and Cinnamon Focaccia

2–3 cups sliced fresh fruit (apples, pears, peaches, and star fruit hold up the best in baking).
¼–½ cup nuts, finely chopped (optional)
½ cup melted butter

Submerge fruit in water with 1 teaspoon salt or the juice of ½ lemon (to keep fruit from turning brown). Drain on paper towels. Brush melted butter on focaccia dough and arrange fruit as a topping. Brush fruit with melted butter and dab with small dices of butter. Top with nuts of your choice.

Nuts and Spice Focaccia

1½ cup nuts, finely chopped
4 tablespoons cinnamon-sugar (1 tablespoon cinnamon to 1 cup sugar)
½ teaspoon nutmeg and 1 teaspoon allspice, mixed with cinnamon-sugar (optional)

¼ cup melted butter
Brush melted butter on focaccia dough. Mix spices and sprinkle evenly over melted butter. Top with nuts of your choice.

Appendix

EASY-MIX SPREADS

Add any of the measured ingredients listed below to 1 cup soft butter, margarine, or softened cream cheese. Store in the refrigerator. If you can, let the ingredients sit overnight to let the flavors mix. Give a good stir and serve.

Savory Spreads

3 tablespoons paprika (Hungarian is good, but may be hot)

¼ cup fresh chives, thinly sliced

¼ cup fresh parsley, chopped thin

3 tablespoons anchovy paste

3 tablespoons prepared mustard

½ cup onion, diced very small

¼ cup blue cheese, crumbled

3 tablespoons fresh marjoram, chopped small

3 tablespoons fresh thyme, chopped small

2 tablespoons celery seeds

3 tablespoons caraway seeds

2 tablespoons fresh garlic, minced

1 tablespoon curry powder

2 tablespoons horse radish

¼ cup olives (black or green), chopped

3 tablespoons fresh basil, chopped small

4 tablespoons fresh mint, chopped small

1 tablespoon cayenne powder

2 tablespoons chili powder

¼ cup honey

½ cup peanut butter (creamy or crunchy)

¼ cup fresh cilantro, chopped small

1–2 tablespoons crushed red pepper, dried

3 tablespoons fresh dill weed, chopped fine

2 tablespoons fennel seeds, crushed

1 tablespoon fresh ginger, minced

2 tablespoons Italian seasoning

3 tablespoons fresh oregano, chopped small

1 tablespoon poultry seasoning

3 tablespoons fresh rosemary, chopped small

1 tablespoon freshly ground black pepper

¼ cup green, yellow, or red bell pepper, diced small (or used mixed bell pepper pieces)

1 3.75-ounce can smoked oysters, mashed with a fork

½ cup smoked salmon, mashed with a fork

Cheese Spreads

Add 1 cup shredded cheese to 1 cup softened butter, margarine, or softened cream cheese. You can add 1 to 2 tablespoons mayonnaise if mixing is difficult.

Suggested Cheeses

American
Cheddar Cheeses
Edam
Blue
Parmesan and Romano
Swiss
Mozzarella

Colby
Monterey Jack
Smoked
Limburger
Brie
Muenster
Port Salut

Sweet Spreads

Use ½ cup to 1 cup softened butter, margarine, or cream cheese plus ½ cup of one or more of the following (chop the fruit small):

Strawberries
Blueberries
Blackberries
Raspberries
Apple
Raisins (or other dried fruit)

Banana
Honey
Peanut butter
Any jam or marmalade
Mini chocolate chips
Granola

MEASUREMENTS AND CONVERSIONS

As I mentioned in Chapter I, I have simplified the recipes and in doing so rounded off all the measurements. These are conversions I found twenty years ago in an old cooking textbook and have used ever since. They have helped on many occasions and are good to know. The first section is helpful when shopping for your ingredients.

The amount	Equals	Equals	Equals
4 ounces grated cheese	1 cup		
1 stick butter	8 tablespoons	½ cup	¼ pound
1 pound butter	2 cups		
1 large egg	¼ cup liquid		
1 lemon	4 teaspoons zest		
1 lemon	2–3 tablespoons juice		
1 medium orange	2½ tablespoons zest		
1 medium orange	6–8 tablespoons juice		
1 cup whole wheat flour	128 grams	4.51 ounces	
1 cup all-purpose flour	130 grams	4.59 ounces	
1 cup bread flour	135 grams	4.76 ounces	

Liquid Conversions

The amount	Equals	Equals	Equals
1½ teaspoons	½ tablespoon		
4 tablespoons	¼ cup		
5⅓ tablespoons	⅓ cup		
16 tablespoons	1 cup		
⅛ cup	2 tablespoons		
⅜ cup	¼ cup + 2 tablespoons		
⅝ cup	½ cup + 2 tablespoons		
⅞ cup	¾ cup + 2 tablespoons		
1⅛ cups	1 cup + 2 tablespoons		
2 tablespoons	⅛ cup	1 ounce	
16 tablespoons	1 cup	8 ounces	½ pint
2 cups	16 ounces	1 pint	½ quart
4 cups	32 ounces	2 pints	1 quart
8 cups	128 ounces	4 pints	2 quarts
16 cups	130 ounces	8 pints	4 quarts

Index